AUSTRALIAN FOOTBALL

Steps to Success

Trevor D. Jaques, MA
University of South Australia

Human Kinetics

Library of Congress Cataloging-in-Publication Data

Jaques, Trevor D., 1943-
    Australian football : steps to success / Trevor D. Jaques.
        p.   cm. -- (Steps to success activity series)
    ISBN 0-87322-670-4
    1. Australian football.   I. Title.   II. Series.
    GV947.J47   1994
    796.33'6--dc20   93-42160
                                                                CIP

ISBN 0-87322-670-4

Acquisitions Editor: Brian Holding; **Series Editor:** Judy Patterson Wright; **Developmental Editor:** Holly Gilly; **Assistant Editors:** Valerie Hall, Dawn Roselund, and Anna Curry; **Copyeditor:** John Wentworth; **Proofreader:** Pam Johnson; **Production Director:** Ernie Noa; **Typesetter:** Ruby Zimmerman; **Text Layout:** Tara Welsch; **Text Design:** Keith Blomberg; **Cover Design:** Jack Davis; **Cover Photo:** Wilmer Zehr; **Line Drawings:** Patrick Griffin; **Computer Diagrams:** Gretchen Walters; **Printer:** United Graphics

Instructional Designer for the Steps to Success Activity Series: Joan N. Vickers, EdD, University of Calgary, Calgary, Alberta, Canada

Human Kinetics books are available at special discounts for bulk purchase for sales promotions, premiums, fundraising, or educational use. Special editions or book excerpts can also be created to specification. For details, contact the Special Sales Manager at Human Kinetics.

Printed in the United States of America

10 9 8 7 6 5 4 3 2 1

Human Kinetics
P.O. Box 80, Kingswood 5062, South Australia
618-374-0433

United States: Human Kinetics, P.O. Box 5076, Champaign, IL 61825-5076
1-800-747-4457

Canada: Human Kinetics, Box 24040, Windsor, ON N8Y 4Y9
1-800-465-7301 (in Canada only)

Europe: Human Kinetics, P.O. Box IW14, Leeds LS16 6TR, England
0532-781708

New Zealand: Human Kinetics, P.O. Box 105-231, Auckland 1
(09) 309-2259

Contents

The Steps to Success Activity Series is a breakthrough in skill instruction through the development of complete learning progressions—the *steps to success*. These *steps* help individuals quickly perform basic skills successfully and prepare them to acquire more advanced skills readily. At each step, individuals are encouraged to learn at their own pace and to integrate their new skills into the total action of the activity.

The unique features of the Steps to Success Activity Series are the result of comprehensive development—through analyzing existing activity books, incorporating the latest research from the sport sciences, and consulting with students, instructors, teacher educators, and administrators. This groundwork pointed up the need for three different types of books—for participants, instructors, and teacher educators—which we have created and which together comprise the Steps to Success Activity Series.

This participant's book, *Australian Football: Steps to Success*, is a self-paced, step-by-step guide that you can use as an instructional tool. The unique features of the participant's book include

- sequential illustrations that clearly show proper technique,
- helpful suggestions for detecting and correcting errors,
- excellent practice progressions with accompanying *Success Goals* for measuring performance, and
- checklists for rating technique.

Many of the activities in the Steps to Success Activity Series also have a comprehensive instructor's guide. However, one has not been developed for Australian football.

The series textbook, *Instructional Design for Teaching Physical Activities* (Vickers, 1990), explains the *steps to success* model, which is the basis for the Steps to Success Activity Series. Teacher educators can use the series textbook in their professional preparation classes to help future teachers and coaches learn how to design effective physical activity programs in school, recreation, or community teaching and coaching settings.

After identifying the need for various texts, we refined the *steps to success* instructional design model and developed prototypes. Once these prototypes were fine-tuned, we carefully selected authors for the activities who were not only thoroughly familiar with their sports but also had years of experience in teaching them. Each author had to be known as a gifted instructor who understands the teaching of sport so thoroughly that he or she could readily apply the *steps to success* model.

Next, all of the manuscripts were carefully developed to meet the guidelines of the *steps to success* model. Then our production team, along with outstanding artists, created a highly visual, user-friendly series of books.

The result: The Steps to Success Activity Series is the premier sports instructional series available today.

This series would not have been possible without the contributions of the following:

- Dr. Rainer Martens, publisher,
- Dr. Joan Vickers, instructional design expert,
- the staff of Human Kinetics, and
- the *many* students, teachers, coaches, consultants, teacher educators, specialists, and administrators who shared their ideas—and dreams.

Judy Patterson Wright
Series Editor

Preface

As part of the annual euphoria of 'finals week', a debate was held on Australian National television arguing the topic that 'football is stupid'. In such a sports-loving society as Australia and at a time when passions are at their height at the climax of the 'footy' season, it was not surprising that the affirmative side was soundly beaten. During this debate, football was called, among other things, an art, a religion, a passion and an obsession. It was described as fast, exciting, rugged, spectacular and fascinating—but it could not be sustained that the game is 'stupid'.

Australian football is but one of the codes of football played in Australia. It is different in many ways from the others, not the least being its uniqueness to Australia. Some would argue that Australian football embodies much of what we think of Australia itself: rugged individualism, brash behaviour and daring head-on aggressiveness. The game is played on fields resembling the country itself—big, open and uncluttered. It evolved when the country was young and of a predominantly male population, thrown together during a time of excited immigration to a new country with few cultural, artistic or sporting opportunities. The large number of Irish making the dash to the Victorian goldfields ensured that the game would have its closest link with the other codes in Gaelic football. At another time or place, soccer or rugby might have been adopted and the world of sport would not have known the spectacular, torrid, free-flowing, running game that is *the* game for so many Australians.

Different as it is, Australian football engenders all that is exciting, good (and bad), appealing and attractive to people who play and watch any other code of football. It has now been played long enough to establish traditions, rivalries and legends—the stuff that ignites passions and fuels fanaticism. In short, it is a great game.

The one word I have not used yet is *fun*. People participate voluntarily in activities because they might be good at them, gain some success and satisfaction from them and because they enjoy them. Australian football is fun. There is much to enjoy about the game. Even the professional players with whom I work, while not necessarily laughing at much of the hard work involved or the devastation of a loss, obviously enjoy their football. If this book in some small way helps young people achieve some success, enjoyment and fun through playing Australian football, then my work on the book has been worthwhile.

Whereas the errors, mistakes and omissions are mine alone, the ideas, concepts and practices contained in this book are not. They are a combination and development of my experiences during many years as a player, coach and teacher. I wish to pay particular tribute to three people with whom I have shared football enjoyment and who, each in his own way, have contributed to this book: the late Howard Mutton, who through his humanistic approach to physical education and football so positively influenced many young teachers; Bob Hammond, a wonderfully dedicated player, an astute and professional coach and now a respected administrator who gave me a chance to relate theory to practice in football at the elite level; and particularly Graham Cornes, a good friend and a great coach who has willingly and selflessly allowed me to share in his and his players' success. The ideas of these men are embodied in this book.

I would like to thank Jack Halbert and Chris Halbert for their continued encouragement and support with the project. Holly Gilly of Human Kinetics deserves a medal for grappling with the intricacies of Australian football from thousands of kilometres away.

But my greatest appreciation is for Trudie, Danielle and Nicole, my long-suffering wife and daughters who are resigned to seeing so little of their husband and father through a football season that seems to get longer each year and is typified by boots drying by the fire, endless football replays on the television and a social life juggled around football practices, team selection meetings and the match schedule. It is to them and all other football widows and orphans that I dedicate this book on Australian football— the greatest game of all!

The Steps to Success Staircase

Considerable debate continues as to the best order to learn the skills of Australian football. Like most sports, practice and the mastery of one skill may often depend on abilities at others. For example, unless the ball can be put in the correct position to mark, it is difficult to practise marking. The steps presented in this book are not set in rigid order (although having possession of the ball is obviously a prerequisite for disposal), but their order is based on some logic. They are not necessarily designed to be separate and discrete. For example, the step on gathering the ball, while highlighting the essentials in learning the various techniques of this aspect of the game, will incorporate other techniques (in this case handballing and kicking) in the drills to practise picking up the ball. This overlap is deliberate. Learning a technique in isolation is not efficient, and techniques are not used in isolation in game situations. Only in context does a particular technique truly become a skill.

Each of the steps includes practice drills, which are generally of three types:

- For the player practising alone
- For two players practising together
- For small groups of players to practise together either at formal training or in free time

The drills are also graduated from simple to complex, with players able to progress from one to the next as their technique improves. Of course, the number of ways to rehearse various skills is limited only by the imagination, and the drills given for one activity can often be used for or adapted to another.

- Drills need to be done at maximum intensity. A player accustomed to moving comfortably to the ball will almost invariably be beaten to it in a game by a player who trains at a greater intensity. To this end, then, you will find my text liberally sprinkled with terms like *attack the ball, take possession, aggressive running, direct approach, confidence, intensity* and *commitment*. Often the drills can be made competitive or more pressured for the player by seeing how many can be done in a set time or competing against a partner either in speed or scoring. Several examples are given, but players should get into the habit of inventing scoring and competitive systems to place themselves under just that little more pressure. What was the score last time? What is the record? What is the score to beat? Questions like these are also useful in setting goals, giving feedback and providing motivation. Practising kicking is valuable, but practising kicking at a specific target (like a post) is more so.

- In today's game players need to be 'two-sided'. From the earliest stages of learning, players should learn and practise the skills of the game on both sides of the body. A player who can kick only with one foot, handball or spoil with one hand, leap off one foot, lead to one side, turn in one direction and so on is not only less efficient and less effective a player but is also easier to defend against. Therefore, in doing the drills, players should vary them to practise in different directions and from different sides.

- Don't be afraid of making mistakes. Careful players play without flair, and only seldom do they 'make something out of nothing' or 'do the impossible' like the truly great players. Place yourself under pressure and don't be frightened of making mistakes. Learn from them and correct them—and in doing so improve your game.

These three points are all aimed at a common goal—developing a committed, complete player, one who gains maximum benefit from practice by pushing himself to extend his skills and who is prepared to do more than exist in the 'comfort zone' of repeating that which he can do at a speed and under the pressure that does not place him or the technique at risk.

After an introductory section including an explanation of the game of Australian football, the book is divided into 'steps', each one focusing on basic skills needed to play Australian football. As you progress through the steps, the seemingly isolated skills become linked so that when you get to the steps on the game plan and positional play, you will be better able to play your part as an effective and confident team member.

In going through the steps you will be best off to follow the same procedure for each one.

1. Read the explanations of what the step covers, why the step is important and how to execute the step's focus—which may be on basic techniques, concepts, tactics or the three combined.

2. Follow the numbered illustrations showing how to position your body to perform each basic technique successfully. Where appropriate, these illustrations are presented in three phases: preparation (starting position), execution (performing the technique) and recovery or follow through (finishing position).

3. Look over the common errors that may occur and recommendations for how to correct them.

4. Read the directions and, where included, the Success Goals for them. Practise accordingly and record your scores, comparing them with the Success Goals for the drill. The Success Goals tell you whether or not you are ready to move to the next drill.

5. After reaching all the Success Goals for one step, get your teacher, coach, parent or a skilled performer to watch you perform each technique and to check off against the numbers in the illustrations as to how well you are performing. Ask this person to suggest improvements.

6. Repeat these procedures for each of the steps. Then rate yourself in the Rating Your Total Progress section.

Now, to begin. Read the section on what the game of Australian football is all about; then take the steps towards becoming a skilled performer and valued member of a team playing this great game.

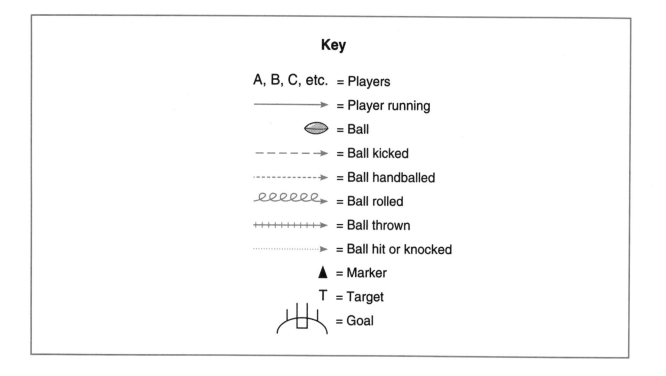

Key

A, B, C, etc. = Players

⟶ = Player running

⬭ = Ball

- - - -→ = Ball kicked

·······→ = Ball handballed

ℓℓℓℓℓ→ = Ball rolled

++++++++→ = Ball thrown

··········→ = Ball hit or knocked

▲ = Marker

T = Target

= Goal

The Game of Australian Football

If you have ever tried to explain Australian football to someone unfamiliar with the game, you know just how difficult it can be. Descriptions often start with comparisons—'It is faster than soccer'; 'It is more exciting than rugby union'; 'It is as tough as rugby league'; 'It requires more endurance and versatility than American football'. But such comparisons are unfair to the game and to the codes with which it is being compared. Similarly, inclusive descriptions fall well short of conveying what the game is. Australian football is much more than a mixture of the vigour of rugby, the skill of soccer, the strength and speed of American football, the high leaping and ball control of basketball and the speed of Gaelic football, even when added to its unique contribution of long and accurate kicking.

A SHORT HISTORY OF AUSTRALIAN FOOTBALL

Australian football has roots common with other kicking sports. When discussing the game's origin, you could start with the ancient Chinese, Indian and Gaelic kicking games. Or you might start with the development of soccer and that famous day at Rugby School when William Ellis picked up the ball and ran with it. Ultimately, the stage was set for Messrs. Harrison and Wills to formulate the Australian style of football. Believe it or not, the game was established to be more 'genteel' with less risk to life and limb than the 'rougher' rugby. However, in typical Australian fashion, the game was played with so much enthusiasm and gusto that it quickly developed into the fast, vigorous, hard-tackling, rough-and-tumble game we know now.

The Australian game of football was devised initially as a form of fitness training for the Victorian cricketers to enable them to beat those from New South Wales. The seventh of August, 1858, is credited as the day the first official match was played in Melbourne. The traditional rivalry between those two colonies has had an enduring effect on the game in that Victoria has remained the strength of Australian football and that, until quite recently, New South Wales, along with Queensland, resisted its intrusion in a major way, and the game played (and still plays) a secondary role to the rugby codes.

The game spread west and south where strong followings were established in South Australia, West Australia and Tasmania. These states, along with Victoria, still are the major proponents of the game, but now it is played all over Australia by more than 500,000 registered players. There are competitions in each of the states, the Northern Territory and the Australian Capital Territory. With the formation of the Australian Football League with teams from each of the mainland states (and perhaps a team from a club based in Tasmania in the near future) competing in the regular 'home and away' games, and with carnivals with teams from all the states and territories at the senior, junior, amateur and schools levels, the game can now be accurately called 'National'.

Although played as the demonstration sport at the Melbourne Olympic Games in 1956, and increased exposure is likely through the Sydney Games of 2000, Australian football is isolated internationally and is likely to remain so—even though the game is seen on foreign television and Australian teams have played recently in England, Canada and the United States as part of an extension of the regular competition. Its relative isolation does not, however, detract from the game, which with its free-flowing style, high scoring, and exciting body contact, will pack stadia and fairly lay claim to being one of the, if not the, most exciting games of all.

PLAYING THE GAME

The game's uniqueness is seen in many ways. It is played between two teams of 21 players each, 18 of whom can be on the field at once. Players are freely interchangeable at any time. Unlike most other field games, there is no offside rule. Apart from after a minor score (called a *behind*) and when the ball is kicked out of the field of play on the full, possession of the ball is continually contested. The field itself is atypical in shape and size, being determined by the space available. It is one of the very few field games not played on a rectangular field or court (see Figure 1).

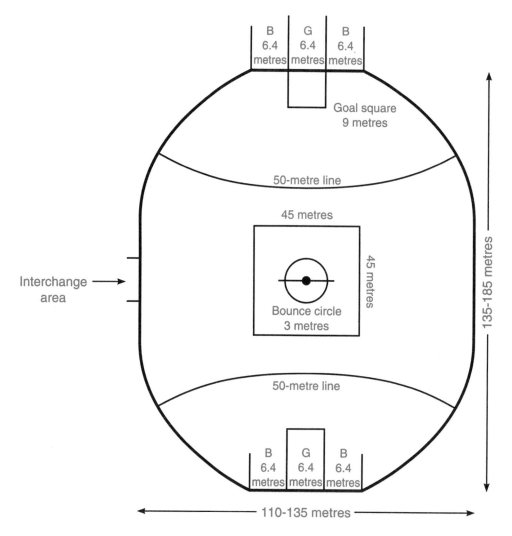

Figure 1   A typical football field.

The primary object of the game is to score more points than the opposition. Points are scored by moving the ball over lines between four uprights, each 6.4 metres apart, at either end of the field. If the attacking team kicks the ball between the middle two uprights without the ball touching any other player or the posts, a 'goal' (worth six points) is awarded. A single point is scored for a behind, when the ball passes between the outer posts on either side of the goal or when the ball has been touched by any other player prior to passing through the middle uprights. A feature unique to Australian football is that players are 'rewarded' for a near miss on goal. This rule developed to prevent the attacking side gaining too great an advantage when the ball was being 'thrown in' after going out of bounds; hence, one point was awarded to the 'scoring' team, and possession of the ball was given to the defending side. Other features pertaining to scoring peculiar to Australian football are that there is no maximum or minimum height of the goals and that a defender cannot score an 'own goal'. In senior games each team often scores in excess of 100 points.

The ball is moved around the field quickly through kicking, punching (throwing the ball is not permitted) and running (with its own brand of 'dribbling' during which the ball must be bounced or touched on the ground every 15 metres). Kicks are often long, covering 50 or 60 metres, with pinpoint accuracy. Catching a kicked ball allows the player to take a free kick if he so chooses, without the risk of being tackled. This aspect of the game adds much appeal as players leap, often in groups, trying to catch the ball on the full, not uncommonly using other players as step ladders to get high into the air.

Each game consists of four quarters, the length of which is determined by the governing body, typically depending on the age and level of the players. In senior levels, the quarters are of 20 minutes playing time. There are no time-outs during the quarters but coaches communicate with players and make substitutions at any time by using a 'runner' to convey messages. If the scores are tied at the end of the game, the game is drawn.

Positions on the Field

One change to the game in recent years has been the tactical positioning of the players on the field. Offensive players will take up a variety of positions, and the defensive players will position themselves accordingly. No matter where the players are placed, however, players in today's game need to have both offensive and defensive skills. There are specialist positions but a feature of a good player is the ability to play many positions. Nonetheless, teams are still traditionally 'placed', and it is valuable for those beginning the game to know what the positions on the field are. Figure 2 shows how a team is usually named to line up. The players will have opponents in the opposite positions marking them. For example, the centre half forward will be marked by the opposing team's centre half back.

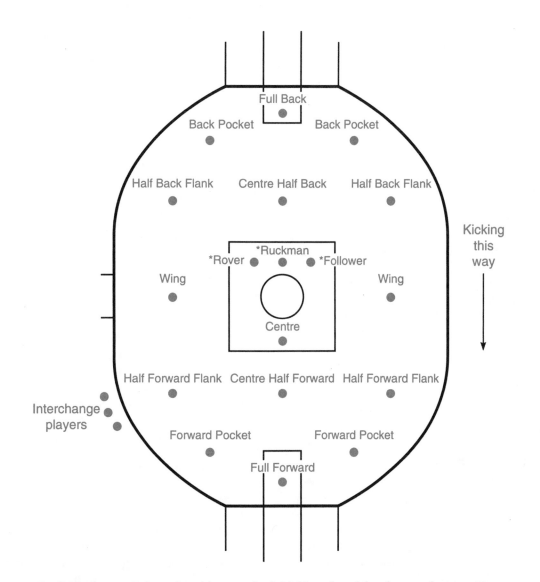

Figure 2   Traditional map of players' positions on the field. The roles of the players whose positions are preceded by an asterisk (*) are to roam the whole ground (they are sometimes called "Followers" as they follow the ball around the ground) and have no set positions as such but may be given specific tasks by their coach. They might change with players from set positions during the game when they may need a rest.

The game is started (and restarted after each goal) by a central umpire who bounces the ball in the small circle in the centre of the field. At this time only four players from each team—usually (but not required by the rules of the game) the centre player, the ruckman, the ruck rover and the rover—may be in the centre square. This is the closest to any offside rule there is in the game.

Equipment and Attire

The most important piece of equipment for the game is the football. It is made of leather, usually reddish-brown for day play and yellow for night matches. The official rules state that the ball should be as close as possible to the standard shape with the size being 570 by 740 millimetres and weighing between 450 and 500 grams. However, children need to play with a smaller and lighter ball to develop correct kicking and handling skills.

The uniform consists of jumper (with or without sleeves), long socks, shorts and football shoes. Each player has a number on his jumper. While each player must have a different number, the numbers worn do not correspond to players' positions as in some football codes.

Shoes are normally of two types. One style has screw-in replaceable 'sprigs' that give greater grip when the ground is softer and the grass long. The other popular style has rubber soles with moulded sprigs, which are generally worn on firm turf and when the ground is hard.

Use of protective equipment is minimal, although some players wear shin guards inside their socks. Although not widespread, a recent innovation, particularly at junior level, has been the introduction of rubberised head protectors. The most commonly used guard is the mouth guard; its use should be widely encouraged to protect teeth and gums and reduce the likelihood and severity of some concussions.

Rules of the Game

The rules of Australian football are not overly complex, nor are there a great number of them. It is not the intent of this chapter to have a detailed outline of each rule. As skills, tactics and drills are described, the appropriate rules will be discussed. Explanations of the main playing rules are found in Step 13.

Most sports have some rules that require interpretation and judgement, usually quickly during the game. Australian football is no exception, and it is here that disagreement and conjecture arise. It is important in making good judgements to keep in mind the spirit of the rules, which have been designed to protect the player who is prepared to go and get the ball and in so doing makes the ball his sole object. Once a player has the ball the rules give him a reasonable time and reasonable protection to dispose of it legally.

Conversely, the defender must not be disadvantaged by any rule or its interpretation to the extent that he becomes hesitant to apply a tackle. Defenders who use skill and determination to meet their opponents and tackle within the rules are rewarded by the rules of the game. So, both attacking and defensive skills are encouraged by the spirit of the rules. Indeed, several rules penalise players who waste time, deliberately force the ball out of play and who do not contribute to the swift movement of the ball up and down the length of the world's largest football field.

At the senior level, the game is controlled by six umpires. Two central umpires interpret and administer the playing rules, and two boundary umpires adjudicate when the ball goes out of play and, if necessary, throw it back into the field of play. Two goal umpires have the responsibility of deciding whether a goal or behind is scored, signalling as such and then recording and keeping the score.

To encourage young players to participate in games and to develop their skills without the fear of being hurt, many junior football associations use modified rules. These modifications may include the following:

- The number of interchange players is unlimited.
- The ball can be bounced only once before disposal.
- Players cannot soccer the ball off the ground.
- A ball kicked out of bounds is awarded to the opposing team (if it is touched before going out, a 'ball up' is contested).
- After scrimmages the game is restarted by a 'ball up' contested by two players of similar build near the scrimmage.
- For the youngest groups, tackling the player with the ball is not permitted.
- To encourage greater participation, the number of players per team is restricted.

- The players who can score are limited, and all scoring must be from within a certain zone.

AUSTRALIAN FOOTBALL TODAY

The game is governed by the National Australian Football Council, which has delegates from each of the states and territories. This body is responsible for the advancement of the game Australia wide. One of the Council's important roles is the development, conduct and promotion of the National Australian Football Council Coaching Scheme. The Council is also responsible for Australian Football Championships between the states. The major club competition is organised and conducted by the Australian Football League. Each of the states and territories has its own league for the games' administration in their area. Amateur leagues, associations and school organisations ensure that competitions are available for all levels, ages and abilities that wish to compete. A recent innovation to promote the learning of skills and the playing of football by younger children is the 'Aussie Footy' program, a joint initiative of the National Australian Football Council, the Australian Sports Commission and the football leagues of the eight states and territories.

Fitness for Football

Australian football is a vigorous game that requires both a variety of skills and a high level of fitness. In senior football it is not unusual for many players to run more than 10 kilometers during a game (in fact, some do almost double that). At times a player will jog but more likely he will need to sprint a distance; then he might have to sprint again before he has had a chance to recover. All of this running is done over the four quarters (2 hours) of a game—so, not only is speed required but also endurance. Players have to chase and be chased, which may involve twisting and turning, and they need to contest strongly in fierce contact situations by tackling and being tackled. They will have to leap, be strong enough to steal the ball away from opponents, kick long distances and be able to fall and recover quickly. Therefore, all aspects of fitness—strength, speed, endurance, flexibility, power, recovery and agility—are important to an Australian footballer.

Although fitness alone does not guarantee skill at the game, without sufficient fitness one cannot achieve full potential as a player. Indeed, some players compensate for deficiencies in other areas by honing their fitness.

The fit footballer has several advantages:

• He may be able to play better. Many of the game's skills require a certain level of fitness. Marking and kicking require power. The player with speed will be able to get to the ball first or to avoid or apply a tackle. Strength will ensure a secure grip when tackling. To get down to pick up the ball requires flexibility. Agility enables a player to dodge, weave and recover quickly from a fall. Skill is insignificant if a player is not fit enough to compete for and take the ball.

• A fit player is able to resist fatigue and perform better for a longer time. Research shows that a tired player's skill, coordination and concentration decrease.

• Fitness helps reduce the frequency and severity of injury. Fit players recover from injury faster.

Although fitness is important, skill development is equally vital—and if skill training sessions are well conducted they will contribute to the players' fitness levels. Conditioning training is not a high priority for young players, particularly the heavy concentrated work required by top-level players. Young football players need to develop the fitness aspects specifically related to football. One way to do this is to practise the skills of football often and under a degree of pressure; this will ensure hard work at both skills and fitness. Fitness activities should include the use of a football and include the football's movements. For example, a running activity can include bouncing, kicking and chasing a ball. Flexibility work can include handling a football. Strength work can entail competing against a partner. And power work can involve leaping for a ball. Combining skill training and fitness training is much more economical timewise (and more enjoyable) than separating the two. Too much time spent for pure fitness tasks (such as running laps around an oval) should be avoided.

FITNESS COMPONENTS

Players of any sport require a basic level of fitness composed of strength, endurance, speed, power, flexibility and agility. The footballer builds on this basic level to develop fitness specific to football (see Figure 3). Football is a game of continuous action made up of relatively short bursts of high-intensity activity followed by periods of various lengths in which to recover. This type of physical demand is placed upon the player for 2 hours; it entails specific fitness that must be prepared for. The game is also one that involves heavy physical clashes and explosive, agile movements; hence these too must be prepared for. Plus, players need to train for their particular positions as well. The rover, for example, requires speed and dash along with the endurance to cover the large field. The ruckman will need strength plus an ability to move all around the field for the entire game. The half forward is at his best if he has speed, agility and spring—skills that must be countered by the half back, who also needs the strength necessary for the strong tackle, and so on. Each individual player will also have special requirements related to his level of fitness, such as a need to strengthen a weak shoulder or to get improved flexibility for tight hamstring muscles.

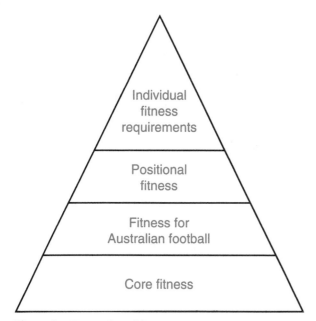

Figure 3 Heirarchy of fitness.

A good way to determine which fitness components a particular player should work on is to make up a fitness profile (see the example at the bottom of the page).

Draw such a profile for your position and rate yourself to get an idea which fitness activities you may need to do.

FITNESS ACTIVITIES

Serious sportspeople will look at areas in which they need to improve and will spend time alone (away from formal practice sessions) working on these areas. Fitness may be an area that additional work can help. It is beyond the scope of this book to detail the principles of various fitness training methods and programs, but some simple activities are offered to give players a start towards fitness improvement.

Flexibility Exercises

Footballers need a general level of flexibility, but they need to be particularly flexible in the calves, hamstrings, quadriceps, lower back, groin and shoulders. Players should select exercises to stretch each of these areas. When doing the stretch do not bounce or jerk but gradually extend the muscle or muscle group until you feel the stretch—then hold that position for about 15 seconds before repeating. Footballers should stretch daily.

Calves

Push-up stretch: Get into the push-up position with your body straight. Place one foot on top of the other foot. Now slowly rock back and try to touch the heel of your lower foot to the ground. Hold for 15 seconds. Switch feet and repeat. Do two stretches for each leg. Finish by putting both feet on the ground and walking your hands back towards your feet, keeping your legs straight, to stand up.

Groin

Sitting groin stretch: Sitting with your knees bent, push the soles of the feet together and hold on to your ankles. Place your elbows on the inner

Fitness Component Profile—Wingman

	1	2	3	4	5	6	7	8	9	10
	(Less important)								(More important)	
Strength						*				
Speed										*
Power								*		
Stamina										*
Flexibility								*		
Agility								*		

side of your knees and slowly apply downward pressure with your elbows. Hold for 15 seconds, relax and then repeat.

Hamstrings

Supine bent-leg stretch: Lie on your back with your knees bent and your feet flat on the floor. Put one hand behind the calf of one leg and the other on the thigh; now flex fully at the hip and gently pull on your calf until you feel a mild stretch. Hold for 15 seconds, repeat and then do the other leg.

Lower Back

Knees to chest: Lie on your back, hug your knees to your chest and curl your head to touch your knees.

Pelvic tilt: Lie on your back with your knees bent and your feet flat on the floor. Flatten your lower back onto the floor, relax and repeat.

Supine straight-leg stretch: Repeat the bent-leg stretch but this time make sure the leg is straightened before flexing at the hips. Keep the leg straight throughout the stretch.

Hip-torso stretch: Sit with one leg extended and the other flexed (so that it crosses over the extended leg) with the foot on the ground alongside your knee. Place the hand on the same side as the bent knee on the floor, outstretched behind the body; place the elbow of the other arm on the outside of your bent leg near the knee. Turn your upper body around toward the outstretched hand using the other elbow as a brace. Hold for 10 to 15 seconds, relax and repeat for the other side.

Quadriceps

Kneeling quad stretch: Kneel on the floor with your knees about 10 centimetres apart and toes pointing behind you. Place both hands on your buttocks and push forward as you gently lean back from the waist to where you feel the stretch. Hold for 15 seconds, relax and repeat.

Shoulders

Standing horizontal shoulder stretches: Stand with your feet shoulder-width apart. Hold your arms out to the sides with the thumbs pointing down. Slowly move both arms back until you feel the stretch in the front of your shoulders. Hold for 15 seconds, return to starting position and relax. Now start with your arms out in front of your chest with the thumbs pointing up. Take your arms out and around, keeping them parallel to the ground. Feel the stretch, hold and return.

Standing vertical shoulder stretch: This time start with your arms to your sides with the thumbs pointing forward. Take your arms straight up past your ears, leading with your thumbs. Feel the stretch, hold and return.

Strength Exercises

People immediately think of weights and gymnasiums when they want to improve strength—but the most available apparatus is your own body.

Arms and Chest

Push-ups: These can be done from the knees or from the regular push-up position. The emphasis with both is to ensure that the body is

kept straight with no sag and that it is lowered to the point that the chest lightly touches the ground; then the body should be pushed up until the elbows are straight in the extended position. When you can do 2 sets of 10 of bent-knee push-ups with 15 seconds rest between, then move up to regular push-ups building up to 2 sets of 10. Regular push-ups can then be made more difficult by doing them with your feet on a chair.

Abdominals

Abdominal curls: These are sit-ups that *must* be done with knees *bent* and feet flat on the floor without being held. Hold your arms across your chest (*do not* put your hands behind your head) and sit up until your back is about 45 degrees from the ground; then lower yourself slowly back to the ground and repeat.

Once you are able to do 30 of these relatively easily change the exercise and place your feet against a wall so that they are straight and about 30 degrees from the floor; then extend your arms. Keep your legs straight as you sit up and try and touch your toes. When you are able to do 30 of these easily, increase the angle of the legs to the floor.

Arms

Pull-ups: Hang from a bar or a tree branch. Your whole body weight is pulled up so that your chin is level with your hands. Do as many as you can before quitting.

Dips: Sit with your back next to a low bench and your legs straight on the floor. Put your hands on the bench and push your weight from the floor so that your arms are straight; then lower the body back to the floor. Work towards your maximum each time.

Groin

Football squeezes: Place a football (or a pillow) between your knees and try and squash it. Don't hold your breath. After about 5 seconds relax and repeat 3 times.

Legs

Stair climb: Climbing stairs is good for strength and also helps develop endurance.

Standing jump: Do a standing jump off both feet to get as high as you can. Reach up with your arms. Do this 10 times with a few seconds rest between each jump.

Bounding: Bound by either taking off and landing on the same leg repeatedly or alternating to take off from one leg and land on the other. Or

try repeatedly taking off and landing on both legs. One set of each of these over 20 metres with a minute's rest between each set should be enough.

Overall Strength

Wrestling: If you have a training partner, a good overall strength exercise for contact sports is wrestling. For example, one player lies flat on the ground while the other tries (any way he likes) to prevent him from getting to his feet. The holding player gives the signal when to start. Change over.

WARM-UP

Before every practice session or game a warm-up will ready the body for what is to come as well as prepare the player mentally. The length of time for and intensity of the warm-up will vary according to temperature, the age and experience of the players and the type of activity to follow. At the very least, even just before a few kicks alone or with a few friends, you should stretch your legs. Then start off with short kicks before gradually making them longer. A general guide is that a warm-up will take 10 to 15 minutes. This should be sufficient time to start sweating, which is an indication that your muscles have warmed enough for action.

Generally, after a warm-up has elevated your body temperature, it should be followed by some flexibility exercises. These are then followed in turn by specific football activities involving kicking, handball, marking and other football movements.

The following is an example of a suitable warm-up that could be done by you and another player (or by a group of players if at a match or a practice).

Activities to Elevate Your Body Temperature

Follow the leader: Have a ball with you and jog around the area bouncing and handballing back and forward. Play follow the leader, with the front person bouncing as he runs. Change over by putting the ball on the ground or handballing in the air for the following player to take the lead. Do for a minute or so.

Alternate foot touches: Stand with the ball on the ground between you so that you both are facing the ball with a foot on the end of the ball closest to you. Now alternately touch your feet lightly on the top of the ball so that each player looks as if he is going to step down on it. But as the foot touches it, the foot is pulled quickly away and replaced by the other. Keep in time with your partner for about a minute.

Sideways jump–sit-up changeover: While one player does 15 bent-knee sit-ups, the other does side-jumps over and back across the ball. Change over.

Roll–handball changeover: Stand alongside your partner who rolls the ball about 5 metres away. Run smartly after it, pick it up, turn. Handball back to your partner and return to your starting position. Your partner gives you the ball and you roll, etc. Have five turns each.

Flexibility Exercises

Lower leg partner stretch: Make sure you have selected a partner of about the same size. Stand facing each other with your hands on each other's shoulders. Both of you take small steps backwards, making sure that your heels touch the ground on each step. When you are at maximum distance apart, stand with both heels on the ground and hold for 15 to 20 seconds.

Figure eights: Stand with your feet a little more than shoulder-width apart, about 3 metres away from and facing your partner. Roll the ball around your body, first one way and then the other, and then handball to your partner who does the same. Repeat but this time roll the ball in a figure-eight pattern around and through the legs. Repeat again but keep the ball off the ground as it makes the figure eight.

Knee lifts: Pass the ball around your body at waist height. Pass it both directions and then handball to your partner who does the same. Repeat several times and then pass it alternately under and over your legs as you walk on the spot with a high knee lift. Don't forget to regularly handball to your partner to do the same.

Twist and catch: Stand about 3 metres from and facing away from your partner. Keeping your feet still (about shoulder-width apart), turn to face your partner as he also turns towards you. Handball the ball so that he can take it in his hands. Both of you should revert back to starting position. Repeat, but this time he will handball to you. Repeat again turning in different directions.

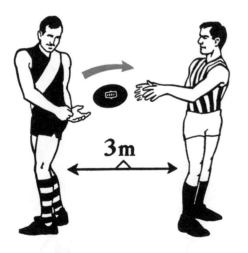

3m

Sitting leg stretch: Sit facing your partner with your legs extended but slightly bent and your feet pressed against the feet of your partner.

Both of you hold the ball as it is held on top of your toes and hold that part of the ball closest to you. Hold for 15 seconds. Try again but with the ball turned so that you attempt to hold it at the ends.

Upper thigh stretch: Lie on your right side and support yourself on your right forearm. Flex your left leg and hold your left ankle with your left hand. Slowly pull the leg back until you feel a good stretch in the upper thigh. Try to keep your back straight. Hold for about 15 to 20 seconds and repeat with the other leg while lying on your left side.

Football Skill Activities

Low gather: Stand 2 metres from your partner and handball the ball at either of his feet. He moves towards the ball, attempts to gather it cleanly and returns trying to hit your feet. Try 10 times each.

Front of the chest gather: Standing as for the low gather, each handballs 20 times to the other alternating the hand used and taking the ball in front of the chest.

Overhead marking: Same as for the low gather but this time lob the ball into the air so that the other can practise overhead marking.

Kicking and receiving: Move back a step or two and practise kicking into the hands of your partner over a short distance. Work on the guiding of the ball to the foot, accuracy of the kick and a sure take into the hands when receiving.

Kick for goal: From about 15 metres from goals or a target, one player stands the mark while the other has a kick for goal. The player who has stood the mark runs after the ball, recovers it and kick-passes it back to the kicker, who is now in a position to stand the mark. The player who recovered the ball runs past the player on the mark to receive the handball and then goes back to take his kick. Try alternate kicks in this fashion gradually increasing the distance of the kick and the angle to the target.

COOL-DOWN

Just as a warm-up is a good idea to prepare the body and mind for practice or a game, a cool-down helps return the body to a resting state after exercise. It is important to allow your heart rate to gradually slow down while still providing sufficient blood flow to aid in recovery. Other bodily functions altered by activity also benefit by a gradual 'turning off'. A good habit, then, is to conclude your practice with some easy jogging followed by some easy stretching of each of the major muscle groups used in the prior activity. These will include shoulders, calves, back, groin, hamstrings and quadriceps (those same areas that had been stretched in the warm-up). These stretches should be done gently, without bouncing. Stretch, hold for a few seconds, then relax and repeat the stretch. The cool-down procedure will aid in recovery if the session has been strenuous and will assist in preventing muscle soreness the next day.

Step 1   **Ball Handling**

Whatever the sport, proficient players practise, and continue to practise, the basic skills of the game, particularly if the game involves a ball. Professional golfers hit hundreds, even thousands, of practice shots just to keep their swings 'in the groove.' The basketballer handles the ball whenever possible—lobbing it from hand to hand, bouncing and dribbling, shooting at goal from many angles and distances. The cricketer likewise handles the ball continually. The legendary Don Bradman spent countless hours hitting a ball as it bounced irregularly off a tank stand.

Although practice alone doesn't make perfect (practice makes permanent—*perfect* practice makes perfect), confidence in handling the equipment does enhance and hone a player's technique, making it easier to develop it into a skill. Because of the odd shape of the ball in Australian football, it is probably even more important than in other sports to handle the ball as much as possible early on, both during instructional times and outside the formal setting. Many AFL footballers, the best in the country, are given a ball each by their clubs to have on hand, and it would not be unusual to see a player just handling the ball at home, at work, watching TV and at other spare times. Watch the accomplished players as they stand and bounce the ball, kick it and then catch it, handball it into the air and catch it, spin the ball, toss it from hand to hand and the like.

WHY IS BALL HANDLING IMPORTANT?

In a game players don't have time to go through the checklist of things that must be done to pick up the ball, to handball it or to catch or kick it. Similarly, as the ball is gathered or marked, it needs to be done cleanly and then moved into the correct position for disposal. As the ball comes, the better player can adjust automatically—hands and body move to the correct position, fingers spread, and eyes don't leave the ball. Such automatic response leaves time and concentration for the other aspects of the game— pressure from an opponent, getting the ball onto a moving teammate, adjustment for the conditions, tactical considerations and the like. Skill and confidence in ball handling, brought about by many hours of practice, are the first step in giving players time and confidence to attend to other things that go to making a champion.

Ball-Handling Drills

Throughout this book in the various steps, simple drills and practices are given to allow you to become proficient at ball handling. The following are some you can try straight away and whenever you can. Don't ever think that you have mastered them. They can always be done faster, for a longer time, in a different position, in a different direction or with something added to make them slightly more difficult to help improve your ball handling. Remember, too, to continually test yourself by devising competitions or scoring schemes. Unlike other steps in this book there are no Success Goals, Personal Scores or Error Corrections here. Just handle a football and get used to its shape, feel and bounce by handling it as often as you can. There is no right or wrong way, and you can never handle a ball enough!

1. Toss and Catch

Toss the ball into the air and catch it. This can be varied in a number of ways, such as the height of the throw or the spin of the ball (end over end away [topspin], end over end towards [underspin], spiral spin, helicopter spin).

The catch can be similarly varied—one hand, two hands, catch above the head, on the chest or as low as possible (perhaps as the ball hits the ground). What about catching the ball after doing a complete turn, while sitting or with one or both feet off the ground? Can you catch it behind your back? Trap the ball on the ground with one or two hands as it hits the ground.

2. Hand to Hand

Toss the ball from hand to hand, varying the speed, height and hardness of the throw and the distance between the hands. Try the basketball hook shot from one hand high to the other.

3. *Figure Eights*

Stand with your feet a little more than shoulder-width apart. Put the ball on the ground and roll the ball around your body first one way and then the other. Roll it in a figure eight pattern around and through your legs. Now pass the ball around your legs and then in a figure eight pattern keeping the ball at knee height.

4. *Bent-Knee Pass*

Pass the ball around your body at waist height. Alternately pass under and over your legs as you walk on the spot with high knee lifts. Now try the same exercise while sitting, keeping your heels off the ground and your knees bent. Pass the ball rapidly around both legs. Don't forget to practise going in both directions.

5. Clenched Fist Punch

Hold the ball with one hand and use the clenched fist of your other hand to punch the ball into the air to catch it. Vary the height and switch hands. Try variations such as always catching the ball in the hand it was hit from. Are you able to spin it so that you catch it always with the seam pointing directly away from your body? Try allowing only one spin before you catch it. You can test this by always being able to see the lacing on the top when it is on your hand when caught. Then add a little difficulty by setting yourself targets of one and a half, two or more spins, etc. before catching the ball. To accomplish this you might have to catch the ball closer to the ground or do higher 'loopy' handballs that spin more slowly.

6. Bouncing

Regularly practise bouncing the ball. This is not a skill used often in games but it is an essential lead-up to kicking and is invaluable to ball handling. The ball is bounced on the forward bottom quarter and should be directed forcefully to the ground by one hand. A proficient player should be able to bounce the ball with either hand. Try to master all of the following (and remember to switch hands). Bounce with one hand and catch with both. Bounce with one hand and catch with one. Bounce the ball as low to the ground as you can. Now bounce it as close to the ground and as fast as you can. Bounce the ball and let it do one complete revolution (backspin) before you catch it. (Is the seam pointing directly away from you?) Even the top players find bouncing two balls alternately (one with each hand) a challenge to their ball-handling expertise. Try it and work towards mastering it.

7. Throwing

Because throwing is not allowed in a game, footballers are usually told not to throw a football at practice. This ensures that practice focuses on the basic technique of handballing. Therefore, with most ball-handling drills as well as the other simple activities in the book use handball whenever possible. However, early on, beginners may find it helps to throw the ball to get different spins, accuracy, distance and power in the movement of the ball. Still, you should practise handballing as early as you can.

8. Handballing

Concentrate on watching the ball, punching it from the palm of the holding hand and hitting it with the flat area formed by the thumb and index finger of the fist.

9. Kicking

The name of the game is *foot*ball, so it's no surprise that players should be continually working on the kicking aspect of their game. A section on kicking is included later in the book, but it is never too early or too late to 'have a few kicks' alone or with someone else to help with ball handling and improving kicking techniques. For example, kick back and forth with your partner. Start quite close together and after each kick move slightly farther apart, trying all the time to kick the ball so it can be caught on the full by your partner. When you are about maximum distance apart, try to kick the ball so that your partner can catch it without moving more than two or three steps.

Part I
Offensive Football Skills

One of the exciting aspects of Australian football is its continual ebb and flow. The ball moves quickly from defense into attack and equally as quickly back again. Consequently, players need to be versatile, able to play both offense and defense. Not so long ago youngsters learning the wing or centre positions were told that these positions were very hard because they required both attacking and defending. This is still the case, but now this emphasis is placed on *all* players in *all* positions. Many of the best attacking moves originate from the last line of defense. Even forward players need to be aware to defend to prevent opponents from mounting an offensive move after gaining possession deep in their own defensive area. It is not unusual for a side to have a good win with their full back or back pocket playing a dominant role. Similarly, forward players often are commended for their team play—not for kicking goals but for fighting desperately to keep the ball in their area.

The statistics in Table 1 are used merely to illustrate. They will vary from team to team depending on such factors as team strategies, game plans, playing and coaching styles, success of the team and playing conditions. Use them to get an idea of how many times particular skills come into play in a senior game. Keep in mind that some defensive skills—chases, bumps, spoils—are not easily quantified. Also, statistics alone do not show the complete picture. For example, how many kicks and handballs found

their mark? The statistics do not include this important information.

Recent statistical analysis of games at the elite level is showing a greater emphasis on offense. Players now run much further during a game than they once did. Players are faster, and so is the movement of the ball. There has been a four-fold increase in the number of handballs per game, and there is more emphasis on playing on from marks and free kicks. Fitness tests on players indicate that significantly greater levels of speed and endurance are required for the running, attacking game now played. Players also have to be able to recover more quickly because the modern game of attack gives them less chance to recover after an effort. The once rare sight of a half back, full back or back-pocket player kicking at goals is much more common in today's fast-flowing, attacking brand of football. The open, running game demanded by today's coaches has replaced the kick-and-mark style and shows the need for players to think offense and to practise offensive skills.

Offense, then, is the name of the modern game. If you don't score you can't win. Attacking the ball, taking possession of it and then disposing of it to advantage is what the game is all about. Note—*attack* the ball and *take* possession. These are fundamental to offensive football. Don't think of *gaining* possession but of *taking* possession. Be positive. The player with the confident—even arrogant—approach to the ball is hard to beat both in attack and defense.

Table 1.   Average Team Statistics per Game (1993)

Offensive skills				Defensive skills		
Kicks	Handballs	Marks	Points scored	Tackles	Shepherds	Smothers
206	147	65	114	41	17	6

Source: Adelaide Football Club

Step 2   **Handballing**

A clearly distinctive feature of Australian football is the disposal of the football by hands. Unlike in other codes, the ball cannot be thrown or handed off. A player can pass the ball in any direction, and there's no limit to the number of passes that can be made. The rules state:

> A Player shall handball by holding the ball in one hand and hitting it with the clenched fist of the other hand.

WHY IS HANDBALLING IMPORTANT?

An obvious way in which football has changed over the last decade or two has been in the use of handball. Previously used primarily as a defensive action when not in a position to kick, handball has now become a potent offensive weapon. Senior teams now handball the ball over 100 times a game—this feature more than any other has increased the pace of today's game. The play on from a mark or free kick (perhaps more correctly it should be called a free disposal), often with a handball, has meant that the ball rarely stops as the team in possession tries to take advantage of the quick movement and catch the opposition out of position. Players should not turn and kick blindly downfield, nor should they hold the ball for a long time while getting ready to kick. Teammates should run past the player with the ball in the direction of their goals and the ball should be handballed to them. So, when a player is not in a position to kick effectively and quickly downfield, he will look to handball to a teammate who is.

It may seem strange that a book on football deals so early with the skill of handballing. But many of the skill practices presented later for gathering, marking, kicking and so on will involve handballing. Also, as I've said previously, handballing is a vital skill and should be learned early, even though it will need modification for youngsters because of the smallness of their hands. Handballing should become an automatic skill for players. Similarly, players should by reflex handball with the appropriate hand as dictated by the 'take' of the ball and the direc-

tion of disposal. Senior coaches demand the 'first give', which means that players need to take possession cleanly in the hands and then almost instantaneously pass the ball off to a teammate. The first give needs to be second nature because of the necessary speed and because it is the only disposal skill where the eyes are on the target and not on the ball. Speed, accuracy and an ability to handball from almost any position (even from the ground, although this is not always recommended), with either hand and over a variety of distances—these are the attributes of a skilled, confident handballer. The slow preparation and pass and the pass with the wrong hand slows the ball and provides opportunities for interception.

HOW TO EXECUTE THE BEGINNING HANDBALL

Footballers are usually advised never to throw a football during practice. Why practise a skill that is not allowed in a game? With most of the ball-handling drills, as well as with other activities in this book, handball whenever you can. What follows are some points to remember when practising handballing.

1. Hold the ball firmly in your hand as shown in Figure 2.1. If held this way it can be moved to any position for handballing. This grip works especially well for players with small hands.

Figure 2.1   Handball grip with support of lower forearm.

2. Watch the ball. As you get more proficient you will watch the target, but at this stage look at the ball, particularly at the spot you are going to punch.

3. Punch the ball from the palm of the holding hand (platform hand). If you don't do this, you are deemed to be throwing it, which is illegal and in a game results in a free possession to the opposition. A ball dropped from the hand is also illegal. A way of practising the correct hit is to grab the wrist of the punching hand immediately after the ball has been hit. Grab the wrist with the hand that had been holding the ball (see Figure 2.2).

Figure 2.2   Hitting from the platform and grasping the wrist.

4. Hit the ball near the back point, where the laces meet. Hit it with the thumb and forefinger area (pad) of the clenched fist. To avoid hurting yourself, be sure to keep your thumb free and not tucked in under the fingers.

5. Get more power and distance by adding body weight to the handball by stepping forward towards the target. Step with the foot opposite to the hand that is doing the punching.

6. Follow through with your punching hand upwards and towards the target after it has struck the ball.

If a player senses he is about to be tackled and he has no teammate to give the ball to, he can handball the ball forward. Punched correctly, the spin of this *tumble pass* will carry it forward where it may be regathered. The tumble pass is also useful to get the ball low past an opponent in front of a teammate. It also tends to bounce higher, making it easier to gather.

HOW TO EXECUTE THE TUMBLE HANDBALL

Point the ball in the direction you will pass it and hit it just below the junction of the seams at the back of the ball (see Figure 2.3). As contact is made, relax the grip on the ball slightly, but your hand must not drop from under the ball. If hit correctly, the ball will spin end over end towards the target.

HOW TO EXECUTE THE ROCKET HANDBALL

Senior players will gain more speed, accuracy and distance with their handball by holding the ball at an upward angle of about 30 degrees and punching it with a firm action just above the back junction of the seams (see Figure 2.3). This will give a backward spin of the ball similar to that of a drop-punt kick, making it easier to catch. This is sometimes given the name of a *rocket handball*.

Figure 2.3   Keys to Success:
Handballing

**Preparation
Phase**

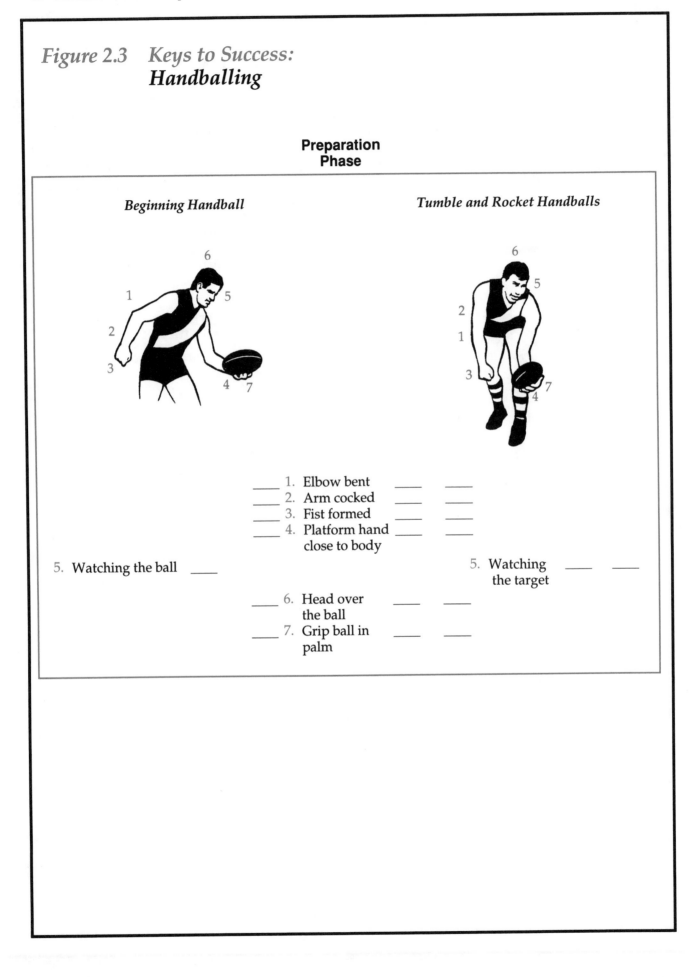

Beginning Handball   *Tumble and Rocket Handballs*

____ 1. Elbow bent   ____ ____
____ 2. Arm cocked   ____ ____
____ 3. Fist formed   ____ ____
____ 4. Platform hand   ____ ____
       close to body

5. Watching the ball ____   5. Watching   ____ ____
                                                    the target

____ 6. Head over   ____ ____
       the ball
____ 7. Grip ball in   ____ ____
       palm

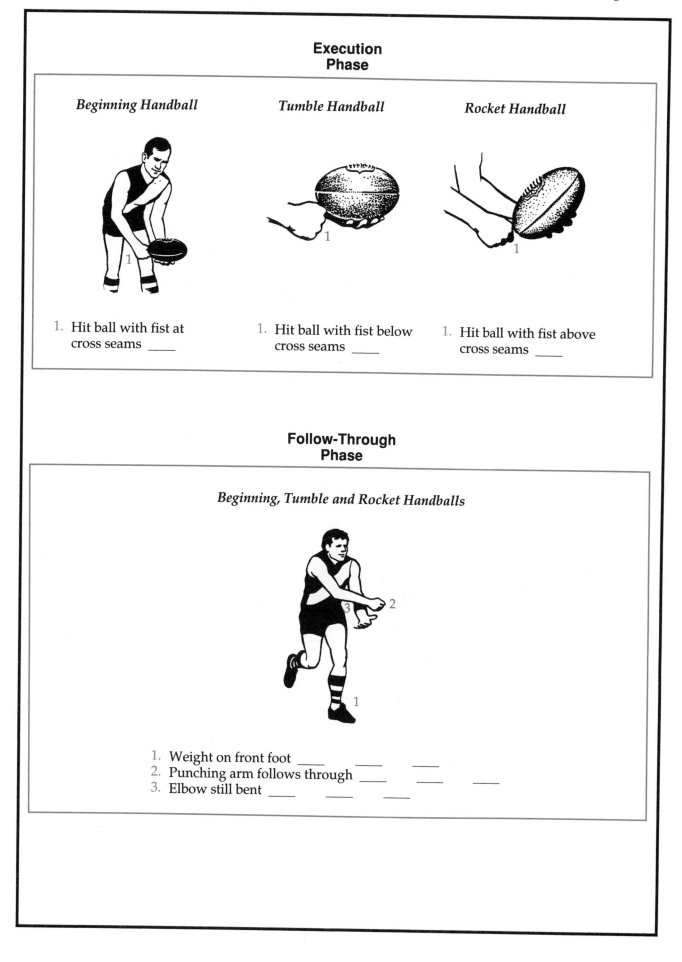

**Execution
Phase**

Beginning Handball   *Tumble Handball*   *Rocket Handball*

1. Hit ball with fist at cross seams ____

1. Hit ball with fist below cross seams ____

1. Hit ball with fist above cross seams ____

**Follow-Through
Phase**

Beginning, Tumble and Rocket Handballs

1. Weight on front foot ____   ____   ____
2. Punching arm follows through ____   ____   ____
3. Elbow still bent ____   ____   ____

GENERAL HANDBALLING TIPS

The object of the handball is to get the ball to advantage to a teammate. This is best done if the ball is delivered to be taken in the hands in front of the waist. To achieve this delivery, experienced players watch the target instead of the ball. However, in the early stages of learning (particularly when passing with the non-preferred hand) players will (and should) watch the ball. Once you have gained confidence and skill in handballing, lift your eyes and look at the target.

To hit the ball with some power, take the elbow back to about shoulder height before striking. Once you have hit the ball, follow through with the punching arm in line with the target. Generally the elbow is bent at about 90 degrees throughout the punching action. (A straight arm leads to dropping the ball, loss of power and an exaggerated upwards flight of the ball.) Power for distance and speed is generated by stepping towards the target. Do this by stepping with the foot opposite to the hand hitting the ball.

The ball should be passed quickly at first opportunity. The receiver should be 'calling for the ball', especially when the ball is being picked up from the ground. If there is a call, the ball can be handballed as early as the player hears the call, lifts his eyes and sees the target. He then handballs 'on the up' rather than waiting to stand upright before passing.

Generally, the handball is made to either a moving player or a player in a better attacking position. Don't handball for the sake of handballing, particularly to a stationary player who would have to turn to move the ball on towards his goal.

Although taking the ball and handballing over your head or shoulder looks spectacular, it is very risky and likely to be inaccurate. Whenever possible, turn your head, shoulders and the ball towards the target prior to punching.

Equally spectacular but also very risky is handballing while lying on the ground. Because it is difficult to get much power this way and often difficult to get the head and shoulders into position, your pass will likely miss its target (especially when the target player is moving as he should be), or be intercepted. Some coaches make it a rule never to handball from the ground after a mark or a free kick, preferring the player to get up, clear the person standing the mark and either take the kick or play on with a handball to a moving teammate.

As with kicking, when the handball is to be delivered to a moving player, allowance needs to be made for that player's speed and movement. The ball should be handballed in front of him so that he doesn't have to reduce speed or, worse still, have the ball go behind him. If the receiver is coming directly towards you, hit the ball easy enough for him to catch it. In fact, you can lob the ball into the air and the target player's momentum will take him to it.

Right from the start, practise taking the bouncing ball (even the high one for which you have to leap) into your hands and then handballing, rather than batting the ball, in the direction of another player. Again, batting might look spectacular when it comes off but it is a high-risk, low-percentage technique that should be avoided. Always take the ball and then handball.

Remember that playing conditions affect handballing, as well as other facets of the game. A wet, slippery ball can easily slide off the fist. In good conditions, handballs of many metres can be made safely and accurately, but when the ball is wet and heavy, the same distances cannot be achieved, and you should adjust accordingly. This does not mean that you should not handball at all in the wet, but you will need to take more care. You need also to consider the wind. Just as a punched drop punt will travel farther and more accurately when kicked into the wind, the back-spinning rocket handball is preferred when handballing into the wind, particularly over a distance.

Detecting Handballing Errors

Most errors that occur when handballing are related to dropping the 'platform' hand, making a weak contact with the punching hand or missing the moving target. These and other problems can be overcome by a return to the basic fundamentals of handballing. Common errors are listed here followed by suggestions for correcting them.

ERROR

CORRECTION

1. The ball is dropped or thrown from the holding hand prior to the hit.

1a. Hold the ball in the hand and against the wrist. Practise handballing while the holding hand rests on the back of another player who is kneeling.

1b. Practise grabbing the wrist of the punching hand with the holding hand after the ball has been hit. You will not be able to follow through as far but your follow through should still be in a straight line towards the target.

2. The ball is easily knocked away or taken from the handballing player.

2. The ball is held too far from the body. Hold it closer with the elbow nearer the body.

3. The player is not able to get much distance or power with the handball.

3. The hitting arm is probably too straight and the fist and wrist not held firmly enough. Bend the elbow, firm up the wrist and punch through the ball. Greater distance and power are achieved with a faster, sharper punch rather than a large back lift with a straight arm. Remember to step towards the target.

4. The handball misses the target.

4. Watch the target and not the ball. Turn your head and shoulders to face the target. If passing to a moving player, make sure that the ball is handballed in front of him. Aim at the waist.

5. The umpire interprets the handball as a throw.

5. Put the action beyond doubt by always following through with the hitting hand so that the fist finishes in front of the platform hand. Exaggerate even this. When practising make sure that you can hear the fist hitting the ball.

Handball Drills

You can do the first three drills in this section by yourself. When you are ready to try the partner drills, here are some warm-up activities you can do. For all of these you should be facing your partner about 4 to 5 metres apart.

- Handball the ball back and forward so that you can catch it in front of the waist.
- Take the ball in both hands and then touch it to the ground handballing to your partner on the up.
- Do figure eight patterns around your legs or circles around your body, then handball to your partner.

- Handball from a variety of positions—kneeling, sitting, lying, after a forward roll or while jumping into the air. By eliminating transfer of body weight by these methods, more emphasis is placed on generating power from the arms.
- Stand with a post between you and your partner. Handball trying to hit the post. If you are receiving be sure to position yourself behind the post to take the ball if it misses.

Note: Many of the skill drills described elsewhere in the book include handballing.

1. Target Ball

Practise handballing the ball against a wall and try to take it cleanly as it rebounds. Vary the distance from the wall and be sure to practise with both hands. With chalk draw five boxes about 30 centimetres square at various heights on the wall. Draw a line four steps from the wall. Standing behind the line, see how many passes it takes to hit every box in order twice (10 boxes in all). Do not move to box 2 until you have hit box 1 once, etc. After every pass move quickly to recover the ball and return behind your restraining line for the next shot. Be sure to turn your head and shoulders towards the target each time. Have five attempts.

Success Goal = Hit the 10 boxes in 10 handballs

Your Score = (#) _____ handballs (the least number in any one attempt)

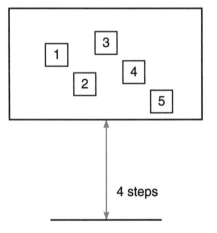

4 steps

2. *Put It in a Bin*

Do a similar exercise but this time instead of a target on the wall use a rubbish bin in the middle of a circle 7 to 10 metres in diameter (put some rocks into the bin so it doesn't topple). Always recover the ball and go outside the circle to handball. Have 25 shots.

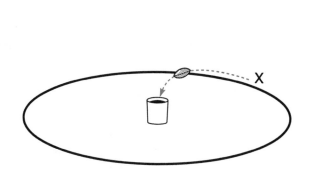

Success Goal = 20 or more bins out of 25 shots

Your Score = (#) ____ bins out of 25

3. *Line Ball*

This drill is designed specifically to practise the tumble pass and to develop power in the handball. Draw two lines 20 metres apart. Stand behind one line and use the tumble pass to handball towards the far line. Chase after the ball and pick it up once it has stopped rolling or gone over the line. Count one if the ball goes over the line; if it doesn't go over the line it doesn't count. Repeat after coming back to the starting line. How many tries does it take to get 10? Alternate punching hands. Do this drill with a friend and you could have a race.

Success Goal = To take only 10 handballs to score 10

Your Score = (#) ____ handballs taken to score 10

4. Partner Target Ball

Using the box targets and restraining line you used in Drill 1 have alternate shots at the targets with your partner. The player who handballs at the target recovers the ball and then handballs back to the other who is standing behind the restraining line. Each box is to be hit in turn (1 to 5 and then 5 to 1). Count the number of shots it takes to successfully make 10 hits.

Success Goal =

    a. Cooperative: 10 boxes in 10 handballs at the target

    b. Competitive: to hit all of the targets with fewer attempts than your partner

Your Score =

    a. (#) _____ attempts you and your partner take to hit the ten boxes

    b. (#) _____ handballs scored by you

        (#) _____ handballs scored by your partner

5. Two-Ball Handball

Three players form a triangle. Players A and B each have a ball and alternately handball to C who has to take the ball and handball back to the person who gave it to him. Count the number of handballs made by C in a minute. Take turns so that each player has a chance to receive.

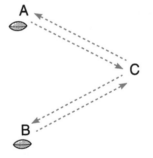

Success Goal = To handball the ball more often during your minute at the head of the triangle than the two other members of your group

Your Score =

    (#) _____ handballs

    (#) _____ first partner's handballs

    (#) _____ second partner's handballs

6. Keep-the-Ball-Away

In a group of four, play keep-the-ball-away in pairs in a 10-metre square area. A 'goal' is scored by hitting a cone or a post or by handballing into a bin. After a missed shot the opponents get the ball outside the square.

Success Goal = To score more goals than your opposing pair in a 5-minute game

Your Score =

(#) ____ goals

(#) ____ opponent's goals

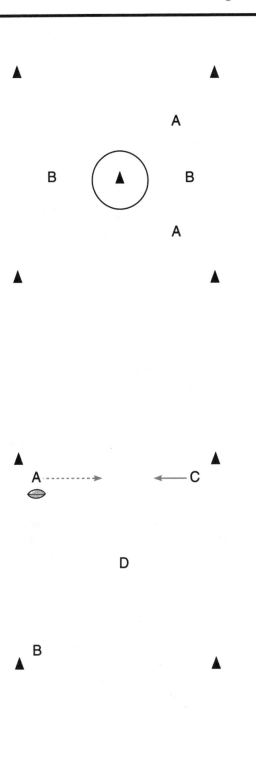

7. Pig in the Middle

Mark a 5-metre square. Three players are in three of the corners and one player is in the middle of the square. The ball can be passed to the corners only *down* the sides, not across the square. The object is to keep the ball away from the middle player. The outside players may (should) move to the vacant corner of the square to take the ball. Change the middle player when the ball is intercepted or after a set time.

Success Goals =

a. To have the least number of handballs intercepted

b. To make the most interceptions as pig in the middle

Your Score =

a. (#) ____ of your handballs intercepted

b. (#) ____ of opponent's handballs you intercept

Step 3   Gathering the Ball

Obviously, before you can dispose of the ball, either by handballing or kicking, you must first possess the ball. One of the highlights of Australian football is that players contest the ball fiercely, whether the ball is in the air or on the ground. By constantly watching the ball and being confident in your ability to handle the ball and 'read the ball', you will make the strong positive approach necessary in taking the ball ahead of your opponent. The ability to read the ball develops by practising getting into the position to gather the ball on the ground, mark the kicked ball or take the handballed, bouncing or falling ball.

WHY ARE GATHERING SKILLS IMPORTANT?

In a typical senior game more than 400 kicks could be marked, allowing an uncontested kick to be taken. However, normally less than a third of kicked balls are marked. Marking is difficult; competition for possession is fierce, and conditions are often adverse. More often than not, the ball is not marked, and it comes to ground. In some situations the ball cannot be marked and is deliberately brought to ground, such as in ruck contests from a bounce or a throw-in or in a deliberate set play spoiling the ball or knocking it on.

HOW TO GATHER THE LOOSE BALL

A common method of taking possession during a game is by gathering a loose ball (one that is free on the ground). Figures 3.1 and 3.2 illustrate several fundamental points to observe in getting the ball from the ground, whether it is stationary or moving.

1. Approach the ball confidently. Expect to pick it up.

2. Keep your eyes on the ball as you take it into your hands or body.

3. Keep your body behind the ball and your head above the ball. If the hands don't take the ball the arms and the body following should block its movement past you and keep it in front. Approaching the ball from an indirect line does not allow for maximum coverage of a bounce to either side, nor does an approach from the side, with a thrust of one arm out to take the ball.

4. Bend from the hips *and* the knees to get down to the ball. This ensures that you are better balanced, less likely to stumble and in a better position to withstand a bump or a tackle from an opponent. Also, if the ball stays low or skids, you are better positioned to cover it if you are crouched. It is easier to quickly come out of a crouch if the ball bounces higher than it is to stoop quickly to cover a low ball.

5. The half-volley take (taking the ball into the hands as it hits the ground) is the most effective for taking the bouncing ball because it eliminates the uncertainties of the bounce. The higher the take, the more variation of direction is possible.

6. It is important to take the ball with the palms facing it, fingers spread, arms slightly bent, and elbows tucked into the body to provide a pocket into which the ball can go if necessary. Young players particularly should try to get the ball into this pocket. As a player's skill and confidence develops he should try to take the ball in his hands to provide more time for effective disposal.

7. Do not snatch at the ball.

Figure 3.1   *Keys to Success:*
Gathering the Ball From the Ground

**Preparation
Phase**

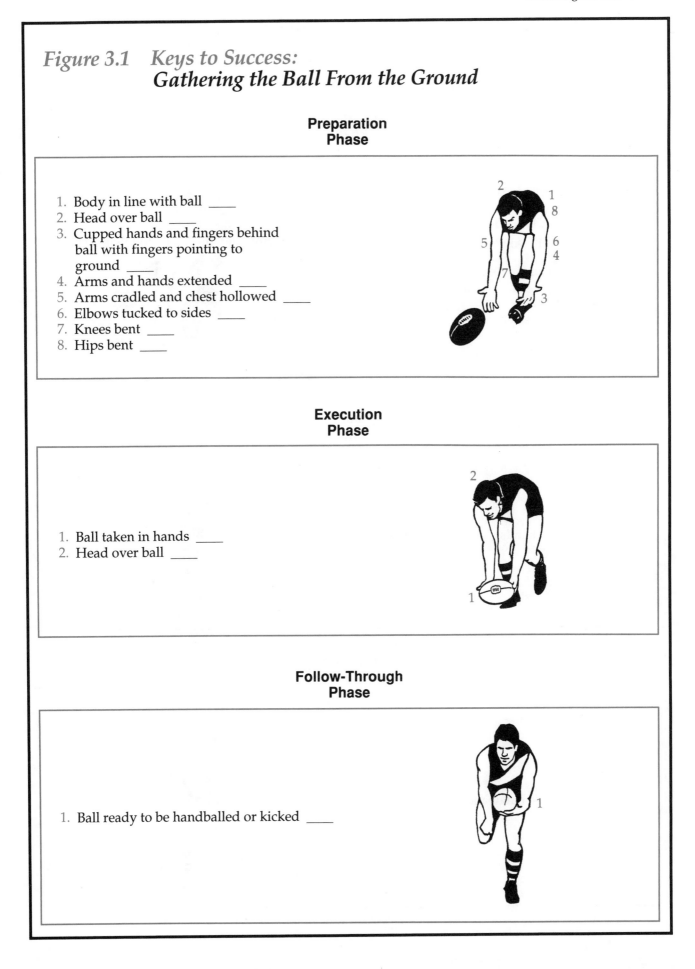

1. Body in line with ball ____
2. Head over ball ____
3. Cupped hands and fingers behind ball with fingers pointing to ground ____
4. Arms and hands extended ____
5. Arms cradled and chest hollowed ____
6. Elbows tucked to sides ____
7. Knees bent ____
8. Hips bent ____

**Execution
Phase**

1. Ball taken in hands ____
2. Head over ball ____

**Follow-Through
Phase**

1. Ball ready to be handballed or kicked ____

Figure 3.2 Keys to Success:
Gathering the Bouncing Ball

**Preparation
Phase**

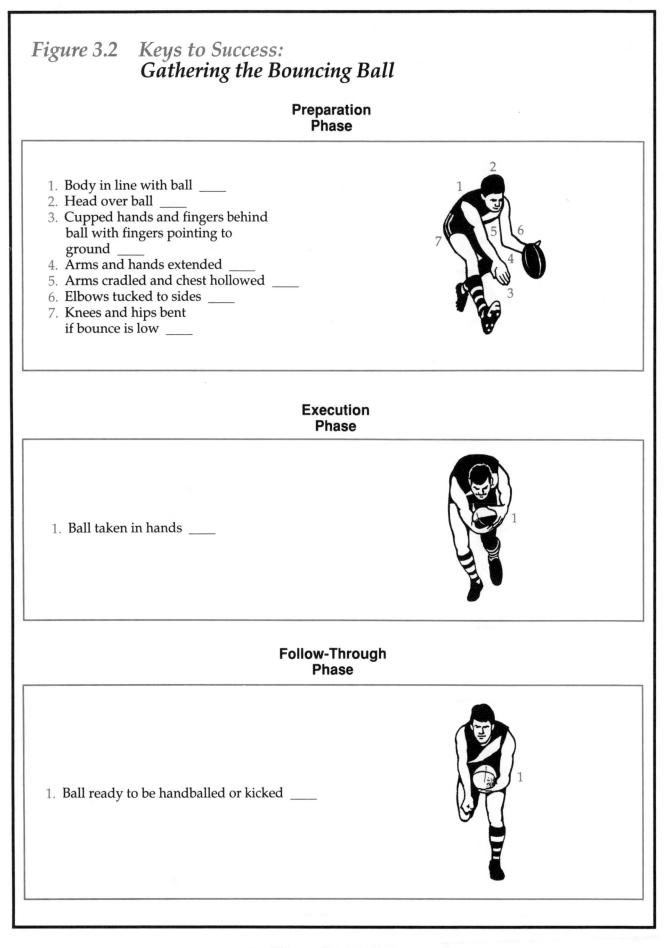

1. Body in line with ball ____
2. Head over ball ____
3. Cupped hands and fingers behind
   ball with fingers pointing to
   ground ____
4. Arms and hands extended ____
5. Arms cradled and chest hollowed ____
6. Elbows tucked to sides ____
7. Knees and hips bent
   if bounce is low ____

**Execution
Phase**

1. Ball taken in hands ____

**Follow-Through
Phase**

1. Ball ready to be handballed or kicked ____

GENERAL TIPS ON GATHERING

Because of the ball's shape, it can bounce any which way. However, we know that certain circumstances will lead to certain types of bounce.

- If the ground and the ball are wet, the ball will hit and skid. When this occurs, your body should act as a backstop to the ball. Your first choice will be to take the ball on your chest, very much like a low chest mark.
- If the ground is particularly muddy, the ball will tend to stop suddenly and stick. In such cases you need to bend low and get your hands and forearms behind and under the ball.
- On firm ground the ball will bounce higher and good judgement is required to pick the angle, trajectory and height of the bounce. Make necessary adjustments to your speed and direction to take possession.

If the ball is bouncing *towards* you, you can generally attack more confidently with your hands and arms acting as a scoop. If your approach to the ball is direct, adjustments for bounce can be made easily.

If the ball is bouncing *away* from you, your approach should be a little more cautious. You might be tempted to knock the ball forward for a more favourable bounce, but this is discouraged. There is also a tendency to bend from the hips only, which might make you stumble over the ball. An approach slightly to the side of the ball with knees bent and head over the ball is better.

A good practice to develop early is to always take the ball and then handball or kick, rather than to knock on the bouncing ball. This practice will lead to better, quicker and more accurate disposal, particularly for the high-bouncing ball.

All players need to know the rule about holding the ball. If the ball is gathered, the player has reasonable time (as judged by the umpire) to dispose of it. He must attempt to do this when tackled. If both the ball and the player are on the ground, it may be safer to knock the ball on (see Figure 3.3) or hit it towards a teammate. Certainly, he should not pull the ball back towards or under himself as he is tackled. In knocking or hitting on, the player does not attempt to gather the ball but hits it, usually with an open hand, into the path of a teammate who is better placed to pick it up and dispose of it. Take care not to scoop the ball up or momentarily hold it, as the subsequent disposal will then be judged a throw, and a free kick will be awarded to the opposition.

Figure 3.3 Knocking the ball on.

Detecting Gathering Errors

Most ball-handling errors in gathering have two causes—not getting down to the ball and taking your eyes off the ball. You should bend at both the knees and the hips to get your arms and body to act like a scoop behind the ball. It is also vital that you watch the ball. What follows are common errors in gathering the ball and some suggestions to correct them.

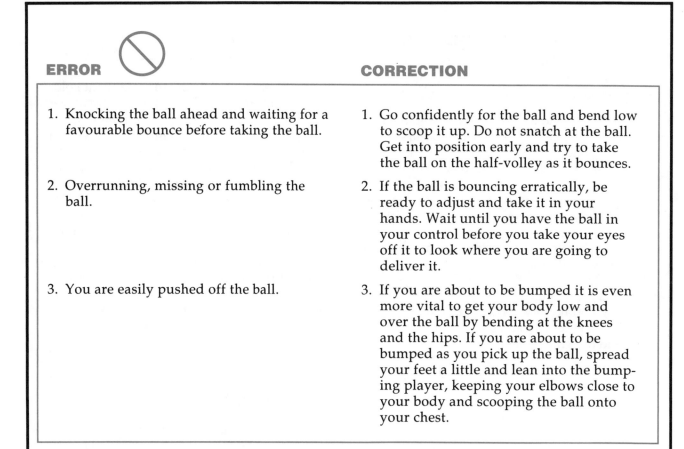

ERROR

CORRECTION

1. Knocking the ball ahead and waiting for a favourable bounce before taking the ball.

2. Overrunning, missing or fumbling the ball.

3. You are easily pushed off the ball.

1. Go confidently for the ball and bend low to scoop it up. Do not snatch at the ball. Get into position early and try to take the ball on the half-volley as it bounces.

2. If the ball is bouncing erratically, be ready to adjust and take it in your hands. Wait until you have the ball in your control before you take your eyes off it to look where you are going to deliver it.

3. If you are about to be bumped it is even more vital to get your body low and over the ball by bending at the knees and the hips. If you are about to be bumped as you pick up the ball, spread your feet a little and lean into the bumping player, keeping your elbows close to your body and scooping the ball onto your chest.

Gathering the Ball Drills

1. Stationary Ball

Practise picking up a stationary ball. Repeat at least 20 times.

Success Goal = To become comfortable with handling the stationary ball

Your Score = Your judgement: How comfortable are you with handling the ball?

2. Rebounder

Throw the ball against a wall and move forward to pick it up as it rebounds

Success Goal = 23 of 25 rebounds gathered

Your Score = (#) _____ rebounds gathered

3. *Roll Retrieval*

Roll the ball away from you and chase after it and pick it up (a) when it has come to a stop and (b) while it is still moving.

Success Goals =

    a. Pick up 25 stationary balls

    b. Pick up 25 moving balls

Your Score =

    a. (#) _____ stationary balls picked up

    b. (#) _____ moving balls picked up

4. *Gather and Shoot*

Repeat the first three drills but this time add a target. Once you have gathered the ball, handball it to hit the target, which should be about waist high. Don't forget to practise from both sides of the target so that you have to use both hands in handballing. Have five attempts at each drill from each side.

Success Goal = To gather cleanly and to hit the target with each attempt

Your Score =

    (#) _____ stationary balls   (RH _____   LH _____)

    (#) _____ targets hit

    (#) _____ rebounding balls   (RH _____   LH _____)

    (#) _____ targets hit

    (#) _____ chasing the stationary ball   (RH _____   LH _____)

    (#) _____ targets hit

    (#) _____ chasing the moving ball   (RH _____   LH _____)

    (#) _____ targets hit

5. *Roller Ball*

Compete to see who is able to gather cleanly the most often. Roll the ball to a partner who comes forward to trap and control the ball and handball it back. Gradually increase the speed and difficulty of bounce for your partner. Score 1 point each time you take the ball cleanly but subtract 3 points whenever the handball back is not catchable.

Success Goal = To score more points than your partner

Your Score =

(#) _____ points scored by you

(#) _____ points scored by your partner

6. Shin Ball

Stand four steps apart and handball the ball at a partner's feet, which are shoulder-width apart. Your partner has to bend and control, pick up and return the ball with a handball to you. Change over after every 10 handballs. Add difficulty by handballing to the middle or either side of your partner's legs. Score 3 points for getting the ball between your partner's legs, 2 for hitting his legs or 1 if he fumbles the take.

Success Goal = To score more points than your partner

Your Score =

(#) _____ points scored by you

(#) _____ points scored by your partner

7. Ball Chase and Gather

Stand beside a partner who rolls the ball away from you. Chase the ball, pick it up and handball back to your partner who then rolls it back towards you so you can pick it up as you return to your starting position. Change over and have 10 turns each for a total of 20 gathers and 20 handballs. Lose a point for each fumble or uncatchable handball.

Success Goal = To handle and handball the ball 20 times without error

Your Score =

(#) _____ gathers

(#) _____ handballs

8. *Gather the Bouncing Ball*

In groups of no more than six, players practise gathering balls bouncing away from them as well as ones oncoming. Players should stand in a row, 15 metres apart from each other. Player A rolls the ball towards B who gathers and hand- balls back to A who then rolls the ball away from B who gathers and handballs to C who runs up to take the place of A. Player A goes to the end of the line. Continue until each player has 10 run-throughs (20 attempts to gather).

Success Goal = To gather the ball 20 times without fumbling

Your Score = (#) _____ gathers without fumbling

9. *Gather the Angled Bouncing Ball*

Do Drill 8 again but this time roll the ball to either side of the gathering player.

Success Goal = To gather the ball 20 times without fumbling

Your Score = (#) _____ gathers without fumbling

10. *Ball Trap*

The ball is lobbed to bounce in front of the player advancing towards it. The player attempts to take the ball on the half-volley and, failing that, to prevent the ball from getting past by covering the bounce with his arms and body. Score 3 points for taking the ball cleanly or 1 point for keeping the ball in front of you. Take off 2 points if the ball gets past. Each player has 10 tries.

Success Goal = To get 20 points in the 10 tries

Your Score = (#) _____ points

11. Defend the Target

Played with one ball in groups of six players. One player defends two cones from handballs from five players in a circle of 2-metre radius. The cones should be 50 centimetres apart. The defender may not go between or leap or reach over the cones. The surrounding players can pass the ball among themselves. Each player defends the cones for 1 minute. He loses a point every time a cone is hit but gets 5 points every time he takes the ball cleanly. The ball must be knocked or handballed back to the surrounding players.

Success Goal = Score 25 points or more in 1 minute

Your Score = (#) ____ points

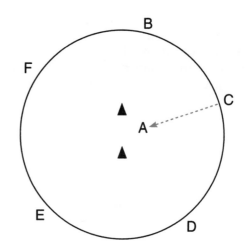

12. Barrier Ball

Players A, B and C should stand in a row about 10 metres away from Player D. Player D rolls, bounces, kicks or lobs the ball quite awkwardly in front of the three advancing players (A, B and C) whose objective is to prevent the ball getting past them. Players A, B and C call to the best positioned player to gather the ball. That player then immediately handballs to one of the other players who receives and in turn handballs to the third player who relays the ball back to Player D. Player D gets 1 point if the ball gets behind all three of the oncoming group. Players A, B and C get 1 point each if they are able to keep the ball in front of the group.

A ———→
B ———→
C ———→

Success Goal = To outscore Player D

Your Score =

   (#) ____ points by Players A, B and C

   (#) ____ points scored by Player D

HOW TO GATHER THE BALL OFF HANDS

A group of players leaping to contest for a ball is called a *pack*. If the ball is not caught and falls from the contesting play it is said to be *off the pack*. Defensive players often will not attempt to catch the ball but will spoil their opponent's attempt by punching the ball. This is called spoiling and results with the ball falling off the pack. An important skill is to be able to read and take the ball off the pack. This skill is practised whenever marking is practised in groups.

Follow Figure 3.5 as you read this list of steps for successfully gathering the ball off hands.

1. Watch the ball.

2. Judge the flight of the ball and the positions of the players before positioning yourself. A ball kicked into the wind will drop short and the best position is to the front of the pack. A ball kicked with the wind will carry and the best position is to the side of the pack to enable you to go either forwards or backwards.

3. Time your move so that you don't move too early and be past the ball or too late and have the ball intercepted by an opponent.

4. Watch the ball come off hands right into your hands.

5. Take the ball in both hands as in marking.

6. When positioning to gather off hands you need to be either close to the competing players to gather the ball as it drops from the hands (Figure 3.4a) or 4 or 5 metres from them to gather the ball as it is spoiled by a defender by punching away (see Figure 3.4b).

Figure 3.4   To gather from a spoil, be close for off hands (a) or a few metres away to gather a ball spoiled by a defender punching away (b).

Figure 3.5   *Keys to Success:*
Taking the Ball Off Hands

Preparation
Phase

1. Eyes on the ball ____
2. Judgement as to positioning and timing ____
3. Be on the move ____
4. Hands ready to take the ball ____
5. Fingers spread. Don't snatch at the ball ____

Execution
Phase

1. Watch the ball ____
2. Take the ball in both hands ____
3. Move away to kick or handball ____

Follow-Through
Phase

1. Dispose of ball by handball or kick ____

Step 4 Marking and Leading

Nothing captures the excitement of Australian football better than the soaring mark, where a player leaps high over opponents and teammates to grab the ball. This is the most spectacular form of mark, but the chest mark is no less important in a game or as a first step for juniors in learning. Good players know when to use what type of mark.

A *mark* is catching the ball directly from the kick of another player who is no less than 10 metres distant, the ball not having been touched while in transit from kick to catch. Once having marked the ball, the player is entitled to a free kick without interference from an opponent unless he elects to play on by kick, handpass or run.

Kicking a ball to a stationary player is generally discouraged because the ball is easily defended against and often intercepted. Therefore a player will attempt to kick the ball so it will meet a teammate who is moving away from his opponent. The moving player is said to be leading or making a lead.

WHY IS MARKING IMPORTANT?

A mark gives the player the option of either continuing on play in a contested fashion or taking his kick free from interference or tackle from an opponent. In kicking for goal or kicking to position in field play a mark gives an obvious advantage. It is equally important as a defensive skill, as intercepting the ball by marking can thwart an attacking move. So, an ability to mark safely and surely is an advantage for all players but particularly for those playing key attacking or defensive roles.

HOW TO EXECUTE THE CHEST MARK

Keeping your eyes on the ball is fundamental to taking possession of it in whatever way, includ-ing the mark. The ball needs to be watched into the hands or onto the chest. Lack of confidence, concern at being tackled or a premature look to where you will dispose the ball are the main reasons for losing eye contact with the ball and making a ball-handling mistake.

The safest form of mark is the chest mark because you can use your body to assist in the catch and to protect the ball from an opponent. In the wet, with the ball slippery and heavy, every attempt should be made to mark the ball on the body (see Figure 4.1).

To execute a chest mark, move confidently in line with the ball to meet it. Your body needs to be directly behind the ball. Do not wait for the ball to come to you because this makes it easier for an opponent to spoil by punching away or intercepting it.

As the ball approaches, your body and arms are prepared to wrap around and cradle it as it hits your chest. Position your arms like a scoop with your elbows bent and close to your sides; spread your fingers and turn your palms towards the ball from beneath. Your shoulders should be hunched as you lean forward to form a pocket into which the ball will fall. Importantly, if the ball to be marked is coming in low, you will need to do a low take—that is, bend at both the knees and the hips.

As the ball arrives, wrap your arms and body around it, with your forearms clasping it to your chest. Keep your elbows close to your sides. In this hunched position the ball should be secure even if you fall or get bumped.

Note that senior, well-skilled players sometimes will take the ball in front of their bodies in their hands, particularly when taking a handball. In fact, some coaches demand this because the ball is immediately in the hands for a quick handball, which is so much a part of today's play on football. However, if you are a beginning player try and take the ball on your chest.

Figure 4.1   Keys to Success:
Chest Mark

**Preparation
Phase**

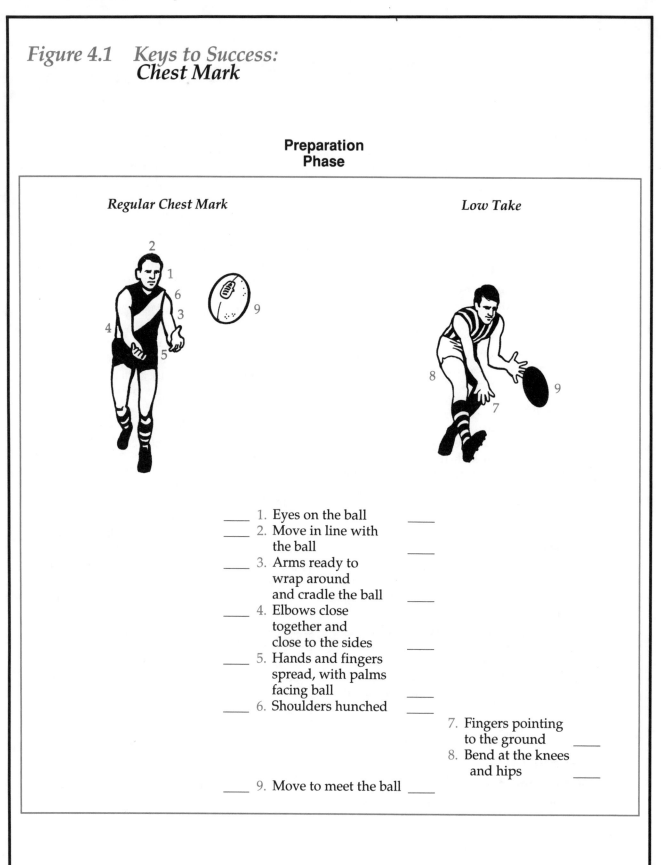

Regular Chest Mark   *Low Take*

____ 1. Eyes on the ball   ____
____ 2. Move in line with
        the ball   ____
____ 3. Arms ready to
        wrap around
        and cradle the ball   ____
____ 4. Elbows close
        together and
        close to the sides   ____
____ 5. Hands and fingers
        spread, with palms
        facing ball   ____
____ 6. Shoulders hunched   ____

                                    7. Fingers pointing
                                       to the ground   ____
                                    8. Bend at the knees
                                       and hips   ____

____ 9. Move to meet the ball ____

Execution
Phase

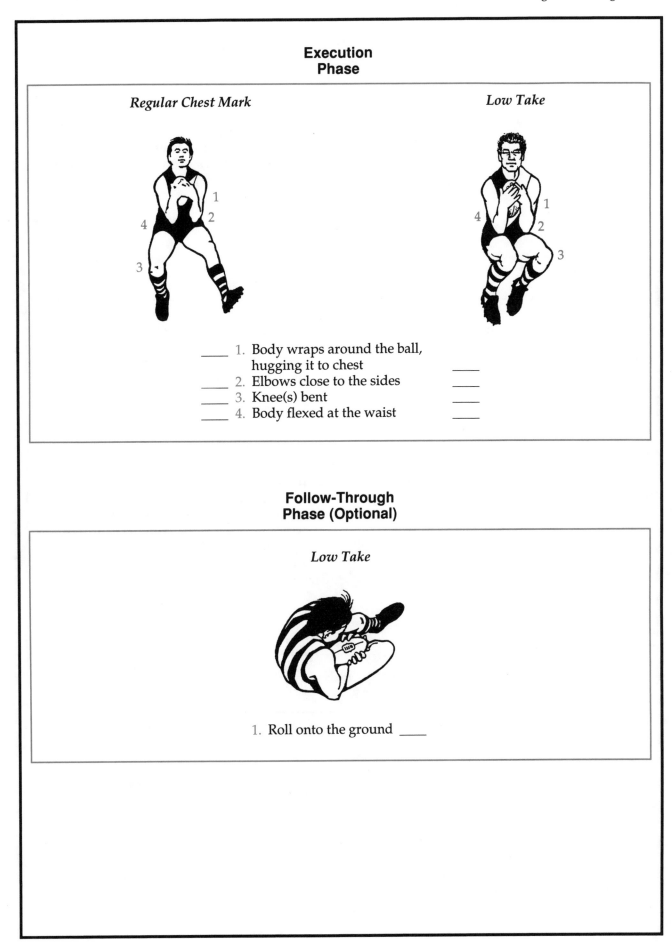

Regular Chest Mark   *Low Take*

____ 1. Body wraps around the ball,
        hugging it to chest   ____
____ 2. Elbows close to the sides   ____
____ 3. Knee(s) bent   ____
____ 4. Body flexed at the waist   ____

Follow-Through
Phase (Optional)

Low Take

1. Roll onto the ground ____

Detecting Chest Marking Errors

Chest marking is the surest way of taking a mark, and the principles of eyes on the ball and going to meet the ball are fundamental to successfully completing the mark. Common chest marking errors are listed here along with suggestions for correcting them.

ERROR   **CORRECTION**

1. The ball bounces off the chest.

2. The ball slides through your arms and drops to the ground.

3. The ball is misjudged or intercepted.

1. This happens when you lift or turn your head away from the ball causing your arms to try to wrap around the ball at the wrong time. Keep your head down and your arms, chest and head like a letter C into which the ball will come. As you receive the ball, wrap your arms under it and hug it to your chest. Remember to keep your elbows close together

2. If you try to 'bear hug' the ball with your elbows spread wide, you will likely lose it. Keep your elbows close together when wrapping your arms about the ball. To make the pocket for the ball deeper and surer, lift one knee up close to your elbows. If the ball is slippery or if you are falling or sliding, it is even more important to form the pocket properly.

3. Approach the ball in a direct line to its flight. Do not wait for the ball to come to you. Move quickly and confidently to the ball.

Chest Marking Drills

1. Throw/Kick and Catch

Using an underarm throw, throw the ball high and then run to position yourself to catch it using a chest mark. Have 10 tries.

Success Goal = Chest mark 10 out of 10

Your Score = (#) _____ catches

If you are confident with your kick, instead of throwing the ball, kick it high, run to position under it and catch it using a chest mark. Have 10 tries. Only count it as a try if you are able to get to the ball.

Success Goal = Chest mark 10 out of 10

Your Score = (#) _____ catches

2. Run and Mark

A partner either throws or kicks the ball to you. You run to meet the ball (do not wait for it to come to you) and mark it on the chest. If the ball is high, leap to take it. If it is low, bend at the knees and the hips. Remember to wrap your arms around it and keep your elbows close to your sides. Have 10 tries and then change roles with your partner

Success Goal = Chest mark 10 out of 10

Your Score = (#) _____ of catches

HOW TO EXECUTE THE OVERHEAD MARK

Every footballer wants to take overhead marks. It is a difficult skill and shows a measure of football ability. Figure 4.2 confirms that marking is a complex skill involving judgement, positioning, timing, hand-eye coordination and an ability to leap, grip the ball and land safely, often while one or more other players are contesting you.

Your eyes need to be on the ball all the time, through the approach, the leap and the take of the ball. Do not drop your head!

Your approach is best made in a direct line with the flight of the oncoming ball, although you may be thwarted by other players. If so, it is even more important to keep eye contact with the ball.

Some marks are made from a two-footed take-off, but generally the leap for the ball is from one leg with the forward knee providing much of the momentum for the flight. This knee also provides some protection for the front of the body and, occasionally, additional lift by pushing off another player.

Early in the leap, lift your arms upwards and forwards of your body. Your arms should be almost parallel as you reach for the ball; your elbows should remain slightly bent.

Aim to take the ball above and in front of your head, where it is easier to keep your eyes on it. Take the ball at the earliest moment possible, when it is difficult for an opponent to spoil.

Your hands should be slightly cupped with your fingers spread and thumbs towards the back of the ball. Your hands should not be stiff but flexible, ready to wrap around the ball as you receive it.

Close your fingers around the ball as contact is made. Your thumbs should be close together to prevent the ball from slipping through your hands. This is especially important when the ball is wet.

Figure 4.2 Keys to Success:
Overhead Marking

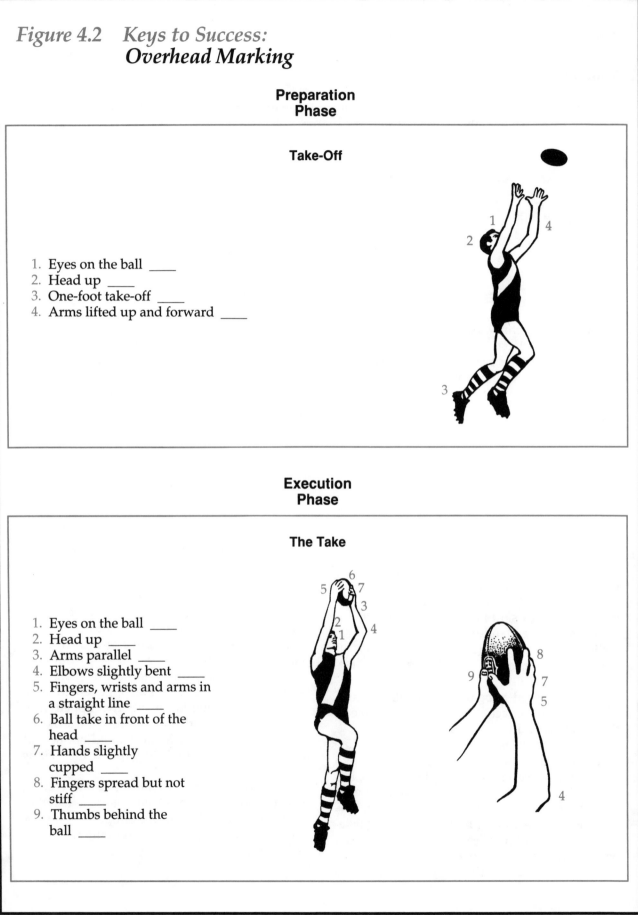

**Preparation
Phase**

Take-Off

1. Eyes on the ball ____
2. Head up ____
3. One-foot take-off ____
4. Arms lifted up and forward ____

**Execution
Phase**

The Take

1. Eyes on the ball ____
2. Head up ____
3. Arms parallel ____
4. Elbows slightly bent ____
5. Fingers, wrists and arms in a straight line ____
6. Ball take in front of the head ____
7. Hands slightly cupped ____
8. Fingers spread but not stiff ____
9. Thumbs behind the ball ____

HOW TO EXECUTE THE HAND MARK

To reduce the likelihood of the ball being punched away by a defender, attempt to take the ball as early as possible and out in front of your head and body. This can be done with relative ease when the ball comes in flatly as you run towards it. The principles are similar to the overhead mark except that you do not leap and you take the ball a little more forward (see Figure 4.3).

Figure 4.3   Keys to Success: Hand Marking

Execution Phase

1. Eyes on the ball ____
2. Arms parallel ____
3. Elbows slightly bent ____
4. Wrists cocked ____
5. Thumbs behind the ball ____
6. Ball take well in front of the head ____

SOME ADDITIONAL POINTS ON MARKING

• Attack the ball confident you will mark it.

• When leading to take the ball on the chest, go to the ball hard. Your opponent will be doing so also, but if you can keep one step ahead he will not catch you and he will have a hard time spoiling the ball.

• Generally adopt the front position when going for a mark. However, this is subject to several factors. If the ball is dropping steeply—such as happens with a very high kick or when the ball has been kicked into the wind—front position is essential. If the ball is carrying, as when there is a following wind, the back position may be better. If the ball holds its flight, the player with a run from the back or the side will have the 'sit' (i.e., the best position) and be able to leap onto the pack going for the ball.

• Judgement and timing are essential in marking. Judgement of the flight of the ball and the positions of the other players are vital, as is the timing of the leap. These are affected by the player's confidence.

• Once the mark has been taken, be prepared to use the ball to your team's advantage. The job is not completed by taking possession.

• Use your voice. If in position to mark, call to teammates that you will take it. If a teammate is in a better position call to him to take the ball. Urge him on strongly and do not compete with him. Remember, only one person can mark the ball. If the ball is within 5 metres you can block an opponent to enable your teammate an easier possession.

• Above all, *keep your eyes on the ball*.

Detecting Overhead Marking Errors

Regardless of how high he can leap or how strong his hands are, the player who does not keep his head up and eyes on the ball will not take a consistently safe overhead mark. Avoid dropping routine marks and take more of the spectacular ones by using basic techniques correctly.

ERROR 🚫

CORRECTION

ERROR	CORRECTION
1. Poor timing and position.	1. Make a positive direct approach to the ball with your eyes on it.
2. The ball drops loose from your hands.	2. Your hands may be too far behind the ball and the ball bounces off them, particularly if you hold them stiffly. Keep firm wrists with your thumbs behind the ball and fingers spread to either side. If the ball is wet, slippery or heavy, the hands come a little more behind the ball.
3. Not watching the ball.	3. Fix your eyes on the ball throughout its flight until it is in your hands. Do not duck your head. Take the ball in front of your head so you can watch it into your hands.
4. The ball is easily spoiled by defenders.	4. Time your run and your leap so that you are jumping up at the ball rather than running or standing under it. Take the ball out in front of your head at arm's length.

Some Basic Overhead Marking Drills

1. Kick and Catch

Kick the ball straight up and as high as you can. Mark the ball using chest marks for the first 10 and overhead marks for the next 10. Leap to meet the ball each time.

Success Goal = Mark 20 out of 20

Your Score = (#) _____ marks

2. End-to-End Marking

Start kicking when relatively close to a partner because the ball needs to be able to be marked so 25 to 30 metres would be sufficient.

For players of all levels, end-to-end kicking is a basic activity for both chest and overhead marking and for kicking practice.

For players who have mastered marking, one-handed marking is a fun method of developing ball skill. This can first be done by chest marking and followed by trying to take the ball in the one hand.

The ball is kicked so that the players have to move to take the ball. Here positioning and timing are added to the basic practice.

Success Goal = To mark more balls than your partner. Each mark is worth 1 point. Subtract 1 point if your kick is so bad that it can't be marked by your partner.

Your Score =

   (#) _____ points by you

   (#) _____ points by your partner

3. End-to-End Kicking (in Pairs)

Here one player attempts to mark from behind another who makes only a token effort to mark.

Success Goal = Not to drop one mark

Your Score = (#) _____ marks

4. Competitive Marking

Same as for End-to-End Kicking (in Pairs) but here both players compete for the mark. This can also be done with the kicker trying to kick the ball slightly to the side of the competing players, so that the player closer to the ball tries to hold position to prevent the other from positioning to mark the ball.

Success Goal = To take more marks than your opponent

Your Score =

   (#) ____ marks

   (#) ____ partner's marks

5. Running Marking

One player kicks to the other who leads to mark the ball three ways: straight ahead, in a side lead and in a drop back to take a kick that comes over the partner. Have four tries at each direction, giving yourself 2 points if you mark the ball but taking off a point if you drop it. If your kick is not good enough to be marked you have to take a point from your score.

Success Goal = 20 points out of a possible 24

Your Score =

   (#) ____ marks

   (#) ____ partner's marks

6. Reflex Marking (for more advanced players)

Facing your partner about 5 metres apart kick the ball so that he has to take it in the hands in front of the chest or face. Have 10 kicks each. Score 2 points for each caught ball. Take a point from your score if your kick is out of the target zone (which is above the waist but no more than head height).

Success Goal = 16 points out of a possible 20

Your Score = (#) ____ points

7. Space Ball

This is a fun game that practises both kicking and marking. It is played by two opponents or small groups. Have a no man's land of about 5 metres between the teams. Each team defends a space of a size appropriate to the size of the group. The basic rules are that the ball is kicked—above head height and across the no man's land—into your opponent's space. One point is scored every time this occurs. The space is defended by catching the ball on the full. Rules can be added, such as only marks in the hands allowed, only drop-punt kicks allowed, no running with the ball, handballs allowed to get the ball closer to no man's land, ball must be disposed of within 1 second of receiving it, players who catch the ball are not allowed to kick it, etc. Play for a set time.

Success Goals =

  a. Score more points than opponent

  b. Score more points than opposing team

Your Score =

  a. (#) ____ points scored by you

    (#) ____ points scored by your opponent

  b. (#) ____ points scored by your team

    (#) ____ points scored by opposing team

X	X	No man's land	O	O
X	X		O	O

8. Marking in Packs

In groups of 3 or 4 about 25 to 30 metres apart, practise end-to-end kicking and marking. Try approaching the ball from the sides and back. How many marks can you take? If the ball is not marked follow it up on the ground, gather it and kick it high to the other pack.

Success Goal = 5 marks

Your Score = (#) ____ marks

WHY IS LEADING IMPORTANT?

When leading, the player is trying to place himself in the best position to receive the ball from his teammates. Generally he is trying to run quickly away from his opponent into a space where he will have less opposition in marking or gathering the ball. Teammates therefore try to deliver the ball out in front of the leading player so that he can mark it on his chest or out in front of his body, making it difficult for his opponent to intercept or spoil the ball.

HOW TO EXECUTE THE LEAD

Do not lead too early. You should not lead before your teammate has possession and control of the ball and is in a position to kick it (see Figure 4.4a).

You should lead into your teammate's vision so that he can see you and is not forced off balance in his attempt to dispose of the ball effectively (see Figure 4.4b). Figure 4.5 summarizes the following points.

The lead can be in any direction—forward, to the side or backward, and can be after a baulk to off-balance the defender. Sometimes the player about to lead will signal the passer as to what direction he will be leading.

The lead should be at full pace. Anything less is too easily covered by the defender. A more experienced player may be able to legally 'push off' from the defender giving him a metre's advantage that is almost impossible to make up. Positioning early is important here so that as the ball approaches, the defender is not between it and the leading player.

Forward players shouldn't lead deep into the pockets of the ground nor to the defensive side of the ground (see Team Play, Step 12).

It is good practice for a forward player who leads for the ball to keep leading even if the ball is not passed to him. Doing so creates space behind for another player to lead into and the ball to be kicked. Once the ball has gone beyond the leading player then he should turn and go with the ball to be in a position to 'read off hands'. If he returns too early he merely crowds the area making the defenders' job easier.

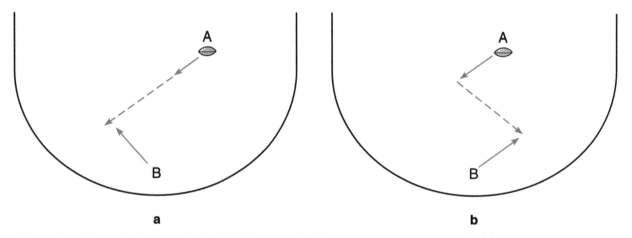

a   b

Figure 4.4   Timing the lead properly (a) and improperly (b).

Figure 4.5 Keys to Success: *Leading*

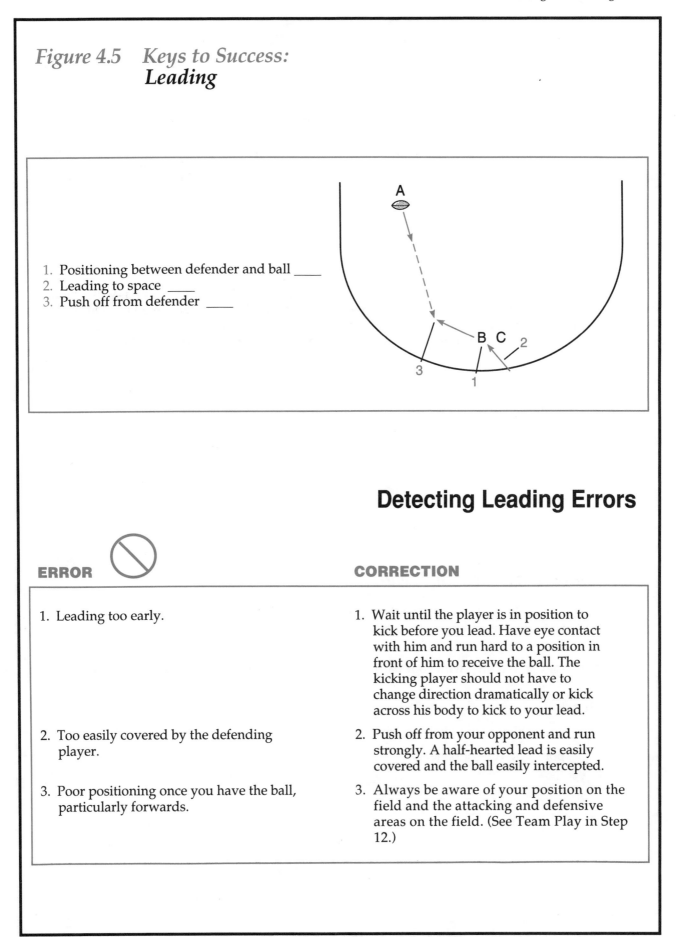

1. Positioning between defender and ball ____
2. Leading to space ____
3. Push off from defender ____

Detecting Leading Errors

ERROR	CORRECTION
1. Leading too early.	1. Wait until the player is in position to kick before you lead. Have eye contact with him and run hard to a position in front of him to receive the ball. The kicking player should not have to change direction dramatically or kick across his body to kick to your lead.
2. Too easily covered by the defending player.	2. Push off from your opponent and run strongly. A half-hearted lead is easily covered and the ball easily intercepted.
3. Poor positioning once you have the ball, particularly forwards.	3. Always be aware of your position on the field and the attacking and defensive areas on the field. (See Team Play in Step 12.)

Leading Drills

It is almost impossible to practise leading by yourself. All these drills are to be done with a partner or in a group. Also, as proper leading requires a good kick, practising leading is also very good practice for kicking.

1. Kick and Lead

Face your partner from about 25 to 30 metres. As he is ready to kick, lead hard in any direction; your partner then attempts to pass the ball to you. Do this as from a mark or free kick. Once you have the ball your partner leads and you pass the ball to him. Both the kicker and the leader get a point if the ball is marked. The player leading loses 5 points if the ball is dropped. The kicker loses 1 point if the ball cannot be marked.

Vary this exercise by signalling which direction you will lead after a baulk.

Success Goal = To score more points than your partner

Your Score =

(#) ____ points

(#) ____ partner's points

2. Competitive Kick and Lead

Same as for the Kick and Lead but this time in pairs so that the kicker has someone 'standing the mark' and the leader has an opponent to push off from and to apply pressure.

Success Goal = Working with your partner to score more points than your two opponents

Your Score =

(#) ____ points by you and your partner

(#) ____ points by your opponents

3. Gather and Kick to the Lead

Player A rolls or throws the ball so that Player B gathers or marks the ball and then passes the ball to C, the leading player. Player C must lead to the appropriate position to receive the pass. This exercise can also be done in pairs with opponents providing pressure to both the kicker and the receiver.

Success Goal = 10 passes received by Player C

Your Score = (#) _____ successful passes

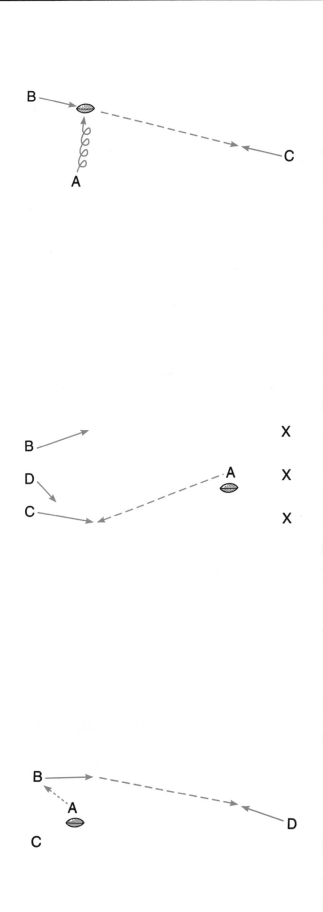

4. Threes

Player A passes the ball to either B or C who have led away from D who tries to intercept. Once the ball is taken, the person with the ball starts the process again to players leading from the other end. Once the ball is kicked, players run through to the other end and change positions so that a different player of the three becomes the interceptor.

Success Goal = 10 caught passes without a
   miss or an interception

Your Score =

   (#) _____ passes caught

   (#) _____ passes missed or intercepted

5. Kick and Lead

Needs four players. Player A handballs to B and C alternately as quickly as possible. Player A chooses either B or C to break away and prepare to kick to player D. Once D sees which of B or C will be kicking, he leads to a position to receive the kick. Change positions after each kick.

Success Goal = 10 passes received by Player D

Your Score = (#) _____ successful passes

Step 5 **Kicking**

Australian football employs a variety of kicks. As the game has changed in style, the most common kick has also changed. In today's game of speed and fierce tackling with little room for errors, we see great emphasis on placing the ball to advantage. Because of this the *drop punt* is now the kick most favoured by players and coaches. The *flat punt* is used as a last resort when a kick needs to be hurried. The *torpedo punt* is used for distance into the wind, and the *reverse punt* for kicking from an extreme angle at goal. Long gone is the *place kick* (now never seen in games). Much to the disappointment of football purists and traditionalists, the *drop kick* and *stab kick* (both where the ball is kicked on the half-volley as it hits the ground) are now rarely employed. With their general riskiness and ineffectiveness in wet weather, these kicks are just not appropriate in today's football, and they will not be discussed here.

WHY ARE KICKING SKILLS IMPORTANT?

Because of the speed and pressure of today's football it is absolutely necessary for players to be able to kick effectively with either foot. Players simply do not have time to get onto their preferred foot. Coaches and opponents know the players with poor disposal skills on one side of the body and defend them more easily by forcing them onto the wrong foot. The better players are those who kick equally well with either foot—to the point that it is difficult to identify which foot is naturally preferred. These players are able to create and use more options for disposal.

HOW TO EXECUTE THE BASIC KICK

Different types of kicks have common elements. These elements are illustrated in Figure 5.1.

Hold the ball firmly in both hands with your fingers spread and elbows tucked into the side to allow the ball to come up naturally in front of the body. Take care to line up the ball, the body and the target in a straight line.

Run forward in a straight line towards the target. Gauge your approach and speed so that you are balanced and looking to where the ball will be kicked. Don't stiffen your arms but allow them to move naturally with the run; your elbows should still be tucked into your sides and the ball held above the kicking leg. Don't wave the ball about. Practise in stages by first mastering a one-step approach to kick, then a walking approach and finally a running approach.

As you are about to execute the kick, move your eyes down to the ball and lean a little over it. When kicking with your right foot, your left hand leaves the ball and is moved to the side to assist in maintaining balance. The ball is *not* dropped from both hands simultaneously. Guide the ball down with your hand from a point in front of your kicking leg in a straight line to your foot; your timing should be linked to the back swing of your kicking leg. Keep the ball in your hand as long as possible. Use both your hand and your eyes to guide the ball to your foot.

Although leg power is important in distance kicking, it is not the only factor involved. Timing and height of contact are also vital, as is a purposeful swing of the leg. The knee and thigh lead the swing, followed by a straightening of the lower leg so that your leg is straight as you make contact with the ball (or shortly afterwards). Swing your leg straight through towards the target, not across the body. Follow through in the same direction to the target. Keep your head over the ball; keep body lean backwards to a minimum.

Strike the ball with your instep (the area covered by the lower part of the laces on the football shoe), keeping the instep firm. In general, kick the ball at about knee height. This will vary, however: The flight of the ball is related to the height of contact. The higher the point of contact, the higher the ball will go.

Do not lift your eyes until the kick is completed.

Apart from the reverse punt, the kicking leg follows straight through towards the target and the player continues to run towards the target.

Figure 5.1   **Keys to Success:**
                Basic Kick

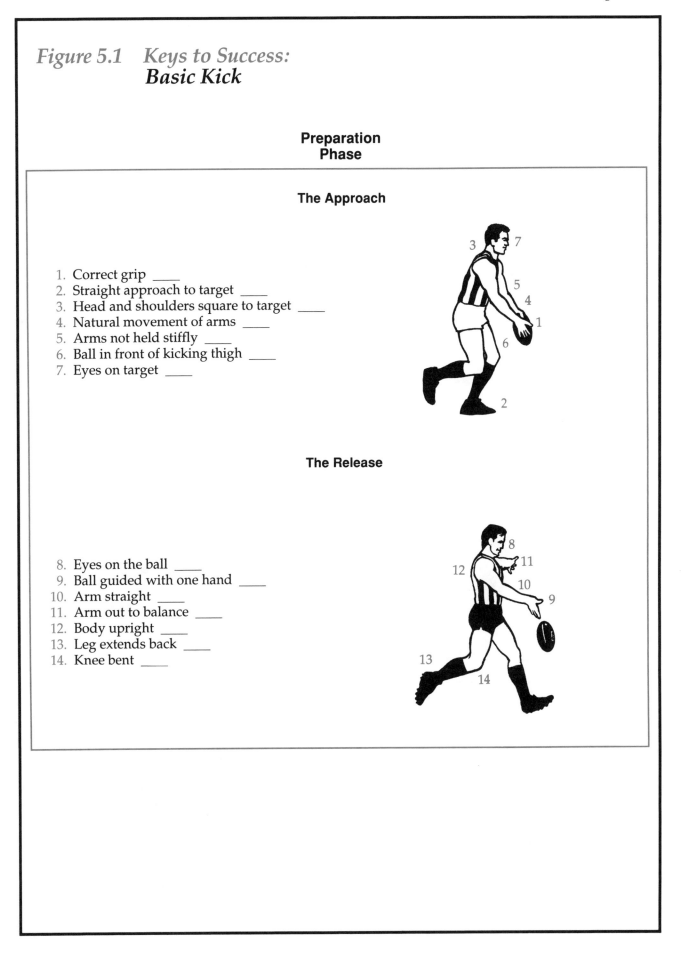

Preparation
Phase

The Approach

1. Correct grip _____
2. Straight approach to target _____
3. Head and shoulders square to target _____
4. Natural movement of arms _____
5. Arms not held stiffly _____
6. Ball in front of kicking thigh _____
7. Eyes on target _____

The Release

8. Eyes on the ball _____
9. Ball guided with one hand _____
10. Arm straight _____
11. Arm out to balance _____
12. Body upright _____
13. Leg extends back _____
14. Knee bent _____

**Execution
Phase**

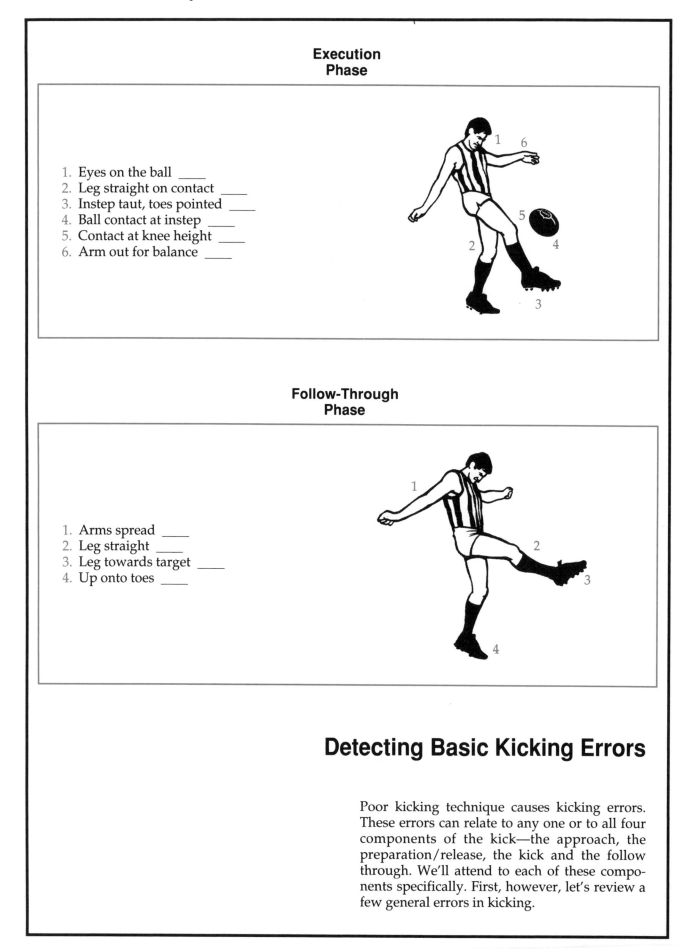

1. Eyes on the ball ____
2. Leg straight on contact ____
3. Instep taut, toes pointed ____
4. Ball contact at instep ____
5. Contact at knee height ____
6. Arm out for balance ____

**Follow-Through
Phase**

1. Arms spread ____
2. Leg straight ____
3. Leg towards target ____
4. Up onto toes ____

Detecting Basic Kicking Errors

Poor kicking technique causes kicking errors. These errors can relate to any one or to all four components of the kick—the approach, the preparation/release, the kick and the follow through. We'll attend to each of these components specifically. First, however, let's review a few general errors in kicking.

ERROR	CORRECTION
1. Inconsistent or poor contact of the foot with the ball.	1. May be caused by dropping the ball instead of guiding it to the foot. Relax your arms; don't wave the ball about during the approach. In the early stages of learning to kick, particularly with the nonpreferred foot, you might find it helpful to hold the ball with the middle finger of your holding hand along the bottom seam of the ball so that you can better place the ball onto your foot. Watch the ball.
2. The ball tumbles badly or floats in flight.	2. This too is due to poor positioning of the ball onto the foot. The ball is turned back so that you kick it at the rear with your toes in an upward movement. To counter this, make sure that the back of the ball is pointed to your throat as you hold it and drop it to your foot. Practise holding the ball with one hand under the ball so that it can't be rotated backwards.
3. The ball goes too high and lacks distance.	3. When this occurs, your foot contact on the ball is too high—above knee height. Don't throw the ball into the air but guide it to the kicking foot and lean over the ball. Do not try to correct by shortening the follow through.
4. Poor accuracy.	4. Approach in a straight line towards the target. Run straight and kick along the line to the target. It is important to guide the ball from in front of the thigh of your kicking leg straight down to the foot. Follow through straight. Do not kick around corners and, when possible, square your head and shoulders to the target. When kicking for goal, aim at a specific point between and beyond the goal posts—the 7-metre gap is too big and too 'comfortable' a target—and run straight towards the target in the approach.
5. Poor distance.	5. A kick's distance depends on a number of factors: timing, a firm foot, head over the ball, contact with the ball at about knee height and a vigorous punch action as the thigh leads the leg action followed by a forceful straightening of the leg.

HOW TO EXECUTE THE FLAT PUNT

Because of its simplicity, the flat punt is the first kick a player usually attempts. During a game it is effective for covering distance when you are forced to kick hurriedly. However, the ball's trajectory is quite high and it tends to float rather than spin during its flight. Consequently, the ball is adversely affected by wind, is quite difficult to mark and is easily spoiled by defenders.

Hold the ball in front of your kicking leg. Spread your fingers evenly on each side with your hands towards the back of the ball and your thumbs opposite each other just behind the lacing. The middle fingers of each hand should be along the seams on the sides of the ball (see Figure 5.2).

Figure 5.2   Flat-punt grip.

Point the ball straight ahead and guide it from in-line with your kicking leg straight to your foot. Make contact at and straight down the instep.

Detecting Flat-Punt Kicking Errors

Two errors are common in kicking the flat punt.

ERROR

CORRECTION

ERROR	CORRECTION
1. The ball will be thrown into the air or dropped rather than directed to the foot.	1. A practical way of trying to overcome this is to practise bouncing the ball onto your kicking foot as it comes off the ground.
2. The ball will not be lined up in the direction it is intended to go.	2. Don't kick 'around corners'. Straighten your body and kick through the ball. Follow through towards the target, not across your body.

HOW TO EXECUTE THE DROP PUNT

The kick used most often in senior football today is the drop punt (see Figure 5.5). It is versatile in that it can be used for accurate goal kicking (in fact it was first used by forwards shooting for goal), a long field kick, a low punch kick into the wind and a fast, low, accurate pass that is not easily intercepted or spoiled. The drop punt is safe and effective in wet conditions, its flight is predictable and its spin makes it the most suitable for marking.

As with all kicks, the height of contact determines the height of trajectory of the ball. In kicking for distance, your point of contact should be at knee level. For shorter, lower passes, contact the ball just above ground level.

Although there are variations in the way the ball is gripped in preparation for the kick, the most common method is to have it almost vertical, with the top pointing back about 15 degrees so that it points toward your neck (see Figure 5.3). Grip the ball with fingers evenly spread

Figure 5.3   Drop-punt grip.

and your middle fingers down the side seams on either side of the ball. Your thumbs are close to the back of the lacing on top of the ball.

Bend forwards slightly from the hips and waist with your head and shoulders kept well over the ball in the run-up.

Guide the ball to the foot for as long as possible and kick it at the back of the toes and the lower laces of the instep. The ball should still be almost vertical. Your toes are pointed (see Figure 5.4). It is the large area of contact between foot and ball that gives greater control, making

Figure 5.4   Drop-punt execution.

this the preferred kick in almost any conditions. It is reliable, predictable and low risk.

The foot kicks through the ball and follows through imparting a backwards spin to the ball.

Because the kick is used so much for accuracy, it is important to make the run-up and follow through in a straight line with the target.

Figure 5.5   Keys to Success: The Drop Punt

Preparation Phase

The Approach

1. Correct grip (see Figure 5.3) ____
2. Straight approach to target ____
3. Head and shoulders square to target ____
4. Natural movement of arms ____
5. Ball in front of kicking thigh ____
6. Eyes move to target ____

The Release

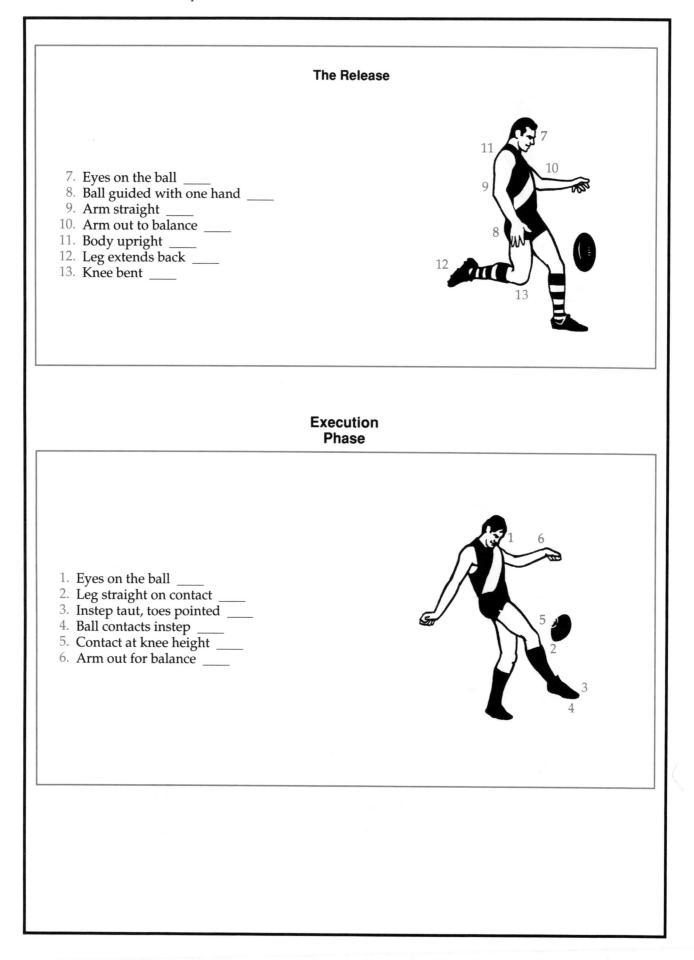

7. Eyes on the ball ____
8. Ball guided with one hand ____
9. Arm straight ____
10. Arm out to balance ____
11. Body upright ____
12. Leg extends back ____
13. Knee bent ____

Execution Phase

1. Eyes on the ball ____
2. Leg straight on contact ____
3. Instep taut, toes pointed ____
4. Ball contacts instep ____
5. Contact at knee height ____
6. Arm out for balance ____

**Follow-Through
Phase**

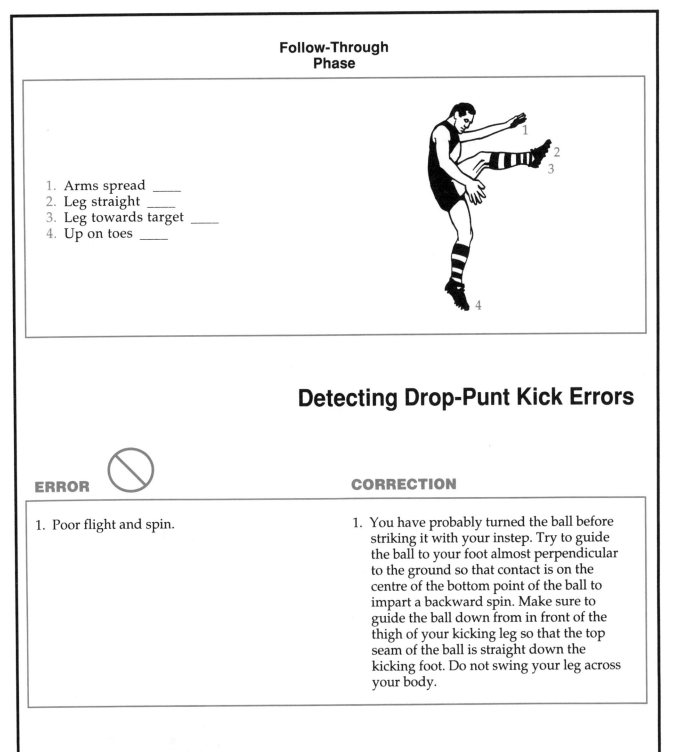

1. Arms spread ____
2. Leg straight ____
3. Leg towards target ____
4. Up on toes ____

Detecting Drop-Punt Kick Errors

ERROR

CORRECTION

ERROR	CORRECTION
1. Poor flight and spin.	1. You have probably turned the ball before striking it with your instep. Try to guide the ball to your foot almost perpendicular to the ground so that contact is on the centre of the bottom point of the ball to impart a backward spin. Make sure to guide the ball down from in front of the thigh of your kicking leg so that the top seam of the ball is straight down the kicking foot. Do not swing your leg across your body.

HOW TO EXECUTE THE TORPEDO PUNT

This kick is also called the *spiral punt*. When done well it is very effective. When done poorly it fails completely in distance, direction and catchability. Because of its high element of risk the torpedo punt is seen less and less in today's football. Coaches discourage players from using it and players opt to do the much more reliable drop punt. So, as with the drop kick and the stab kick, the torpedo punt will likely soon be consigned to the coaching manuals and pictures and videos of the 'golden oldies'.

When kicking a torpedo punt, guide the ball to your foot so that it angles across the foot on contact. This imparts a longitudinal spin to the ball that makes this kick effective when the ball is kicked into the wind or needs to gain distance.

The spin also curves the ball's flight—which can be an advantage in some goal attempts, but which makes it difficult to use for passing. As shown in Figure 5.6, the direction of the curve depends on which foot the ball is kicked with. The torpedo punt is easier to mark than the flat punt but is not as much preferred as the drop punt.

Figure 5.6   Right-foot kick (a) and left-foot kick (b).

Figure 5.7 illustrates how to execute the torpedo punt. For a right-foot kick, hold the ball with fingers spread on each side and slightly on top with your left hand slightly in front of the lacing and the right hand just behind. This makes the angle of the ball to the target about 10 to 15 degrees.

Guide the ball to your foot with the right hand and contact it at about knee height with the ball at an angle of about 15 degrees to the ground. The ball begins to spiral when contact is made by the lower part of the instep at a slight angle across the foot. Note that the ball is *not* kicked with the side of the foot.

Figure 5.7   Keys to Success: *The Torpedo Punt*

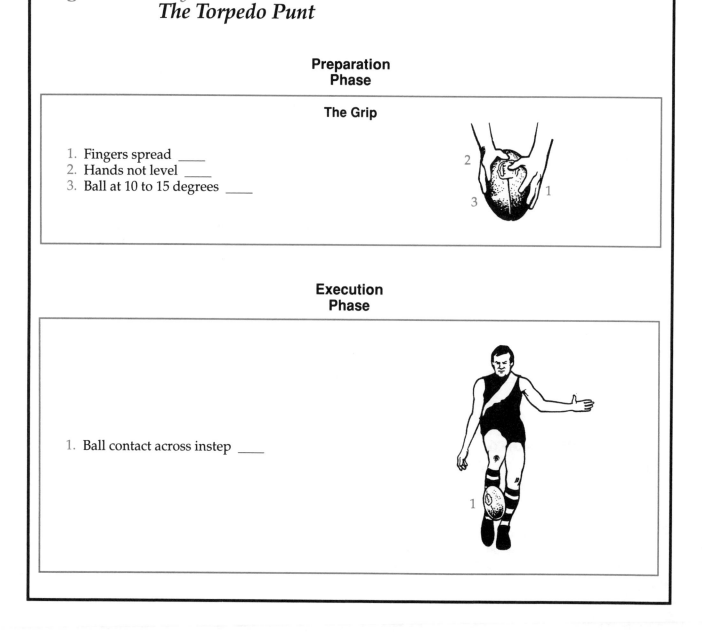

Preparation Phase

The Grip

1. Fingers spread ____
2. Hands not level ____
3. Ball at 10 to 15 degrees ____

Execution Phase

1. Ball contact across instep ____

Follow-Through
Phase

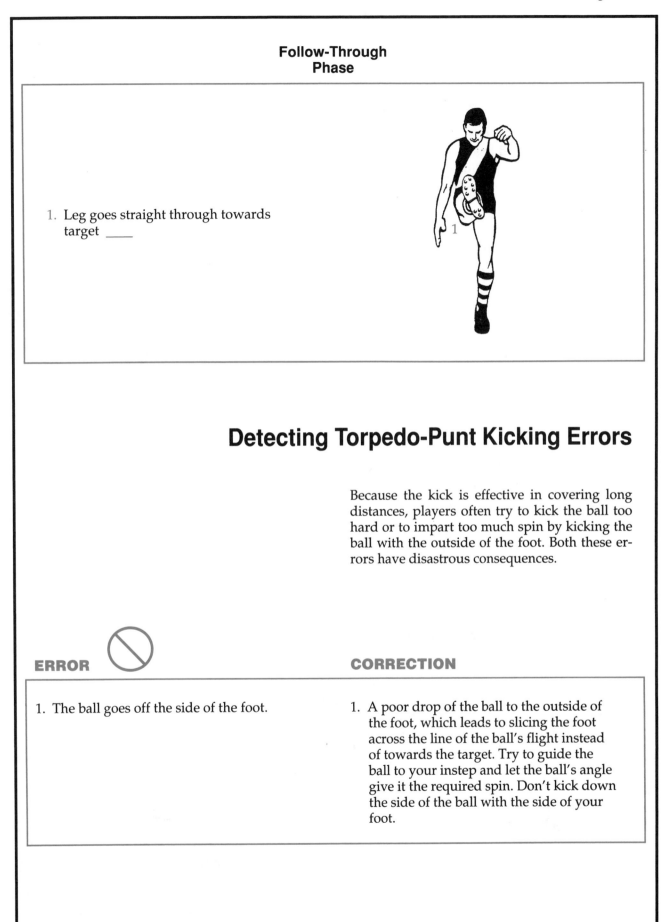

1. Leg goes straight through towards target ____

Detecting Torpedo-Punt Kicking Errors

Because the kick is effective in covering long distances, players often try to kick the ball too hard or to impart too much spin by kicking the ball with the outside of the foot. Both these errors have disastrous consequences.

ERROR

CORRECTION

1. The ball goes off the side of the foot.

1. A poor drop of the ball to the outside of the foot, which leads to slicing the foot across the line of the ball's flight instead of towards the target. Try to guide the ball to your instep and let the ball's angle give it the required spin. Don't kick down the side of the ball with the side of your foot.

HOW TO EXECUTE THE REVERSE PUNT

During games the attacking team tries to position the ball in front of the goals at an angle that allows a relatively easy kick to score. Good defense will prevent the centering of the ball, and a player may be forced to shoot for goal from a tough angle. He can try to improve his chances by using a kick with a curved flight. For instance, a right-foot player may try a torpedo-punt kick from the left side of the goals.

A right-foot player from the right side may attempt to use a reverse punt. To do so he will aim at the imaginary target (T) and use the reverse curve to kick the goal (see Figure 5.8).

Figure 5.8   Flight of the ball for the reverse punt.

The reverse punt (illustrated in Figure 5.9) has proven successful not only in kicking for goal but also in field play when the player is caught 'on the wrong foot' and needs to get the ball away at an angle to a teammate. This carries a high element of risk, however, and should be seen only as a desperate measure. Players are better served by learning to kick with both feet.

Hold the ball end to end at about 45 degrees to the line to the target with the guiding hand holding the front of the ball.

Hold the ball so that when it is released it will contact your foot almost parallel to the ground.

Run in a straight line towards your imaginary target.

Kick the ball with your instep, using your judgement about the point of contact. The further away from the centre of the ball that contact is made, the greater the angle from the line to the imaginary target will the ball diverge. The greater the distance required, the closer to the middle of the ball should contact be made.

In the follow through, your leg slices behind the ball on contact and moves slightly away in the direction opposite the ball's flight.

Figure 5.9   Keys to Success: The Reverse Punt

Preparation Phase

The Grip

1. Ball at 45° ____
2. Guiding hand forward ____

Execution
Phase

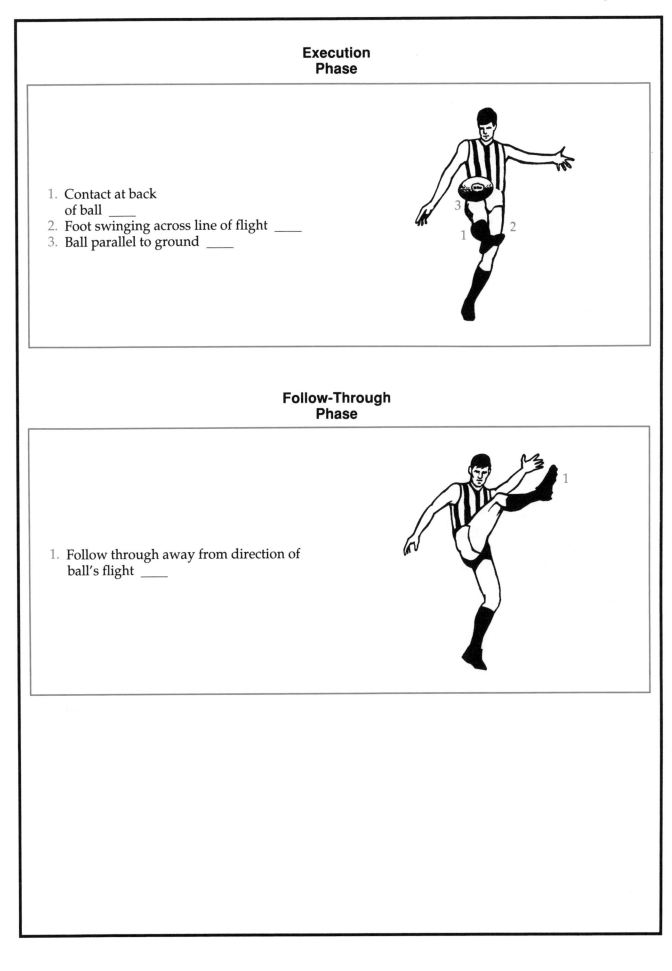

1. Contact at back
   of ball ____
2. Foot swinging across line of flight ____
3. Ball parallel to ground ____

Follow-Through
Phase

1. Follow through away from direction of
   ball's flight ____

Detecting Reverse-Punt Kick Errors

ERROR ⊘	CORRECTION
1. The reverse punt is not easy to execute. The major problem is in gauging the angle required for the curved flight.	1. If the angle is too narrow, the ball will fly past the goals; if it is too sharp, the ball will fall short of the goal. Identifying an imaginary target to run and kick towards is a matter of practice. Once you have picked the target, try to ignore the goal posts.

SOME GENERAL POINTS ON KICKING

Keep the following tips in mind as you practise your kicking skills:

• When possible, straighten your run and your body so that your leg swing and follow through is straight at the target. It helps to get your eyes and shoulders square with the target. Try to avoid 'kicking around corners'.

• When kicking to a moving player aim at a space in front of the player to allow him to take the ball in front, making it easier for him to play on and more difficult for a defender to spoil.

• To keep the ball low (when passing or when punching the ball into the wind), keep your shoulders and head over the ball and strike the ball at a lower point.

• When kicking for distance there is a tendency to rock back so that your kicking leg can straighten earlier, make contact higher and provide greater power. However, the amount of back body lean should be minimised, as greater distance is achieved by better timing with a larger backswing.

• In kicking for goal, particularly from a set shot, narrow the target by picking a spot between and beyond the goal posts at which to aim. It might also help to scratch a mark on the ground near where the ball is marked; then when you go back to take the kick, keep the mark directly between you and the goals to guide you in the run-up.

Some Kicking Drills

Though almost all drills can involve kicking, some are best specifically for kicking practice. Most of the following drills can be used for all types of kick except for the reverse punt, which is usually only practised by kicking at goal from near the boundary line.

1. Pair Kicking

In pairs about 10 to 15 metres apart kick to your partner (and he to you) while checking for correct technique.

A very good drill to ensure placement of the ball onto the foot and to develop some power for the kick is to kick over a short distance, say 4 to 5 metres, and not to step at all. Only the kicking leg moves. Have your partner tell you whether the ball was guided to the foot, if it was pointing in the right direction and about the technique of the follow through.

Success Goal = 20 kicks correctly executed and received

Your Score = (#) ____ kicks correctly executed and received

2. Square Ball

Now increase the space between you and your partner and kick for distance. First kick high and long. Then try low and long kicks. You can make this competitive by playing 'Square Ball'. Have two 5-metre squares 30 to 35 metres apart (closer for younger players). From one square kick to your partner who is standing in the other. Score as follows: 3 points if the ball can be marked by your partners, 2 points if he takes it with one foot in the square and 1 point if it bounces into the square. Take 3 points *off* your score if you drop one of your partner's kicks that comes into your square. Have 10 kicks each.

Success Goal = To score more than 25 points out of a possible 30

Your Score =

(#) ____ your points

(#) ____ points by your partner

Vary this drill by having the receiver stand 10 metres outside the square as the ball is kicked and then run into the square to take the mark. This drill is designed to practise kicking in front of the moving player. Have another 10 kicks each.

Success Goal = To score more than 25 points out of a possible 30

Your Score =

(#) ____ your points

(#) ____ points by your partner

3. Competitive Goal Scoring

Place 10 markers at various distances and angles from the goal. Each player will have one shot at goal from each of the markers in the following fashion. Player A takes the first kick. Player B stands with hands in the air at the first marker (this is called *standing the mark*). Player A kicks at goal over player B and gets 6 points for a goal or 1 point for a behind. Player B immediately sprints after the ball, recovers it and kicks it to A, who has moved to the marker. Player B runs back past A who handballs to B. Player B now takes the kick for goal. Player A recovers the ball and passes it back to B who has moved onto the second marker, and so on.

Success Goals =

   a. To score 10 goals

   b. To score more points than your partner

Your Score =

   a. (#) ____ goals

   b. (#) ____ goals by you

     (#) ____ goals by your partner

4. Kicking to the Lead

From both standing and running starts, kick the ball to a leading partner. Concentrate on kicking to the front of the movement. Have the leading player come from a variety of angles—towards, from the side, dropping back.

Success Goal = 17 out of a possible 20 completed passes

Your Score = (#) ____ completed passes

5. *Target Ball*

Practise kicking at stationary targets such as the goal and behind posts, the gate, cones and specially built targets. Too often the receiver makes the kick 'look good' because he makes position to receive the ball and is able to adjust pace, position and distance so that a less than perfect kick looks good. A good way to get feedback on your accuracy is to kick to players who are directed not to move. If they can catch the ball without moving from their positions, you know you have kicked accurately.

In groups of four form up in relay fashion, two at either end 30 metres apart. The ball is kicked to the receiver with scoring as follows:

- 4 points if the receiver can catch the ball without moving his feet
- 3 points if the receiver jumps into the air to take the ball above his head
- 2 points if the receiver can take the ball but must take one step (in any direction) to do so
- 1 point if the player has to move both feet to take the ball
- 0 points if the ball can't be caught

The kicker runs through and touches the receiver on the shoulder. The receiver then moves off to kick to the other end. Continue until every player has had 10 kicks. Who got the greatest score?

Success Goal = To score more than 30 points

Your Score = (#) _____ points

6. Pressure Kicking

For three players. Have some markers near a wall be a 'goal'. Place a kicking marker about 25 metres away. Player A handballs to B who is running fast from the marker and is chased by C who tries to put two hands on B to simulate a tackle. Player B has a running shot at goal and scores a point for every goal. Player B recovers the ball, A becomes the chaser and C the kicker. Have 10 tries each at kicking for goal under pressure.

Success Goal = To score 10 goals from 10 shots

Your Score =

   (#) _____ goals scored by you

   (#) _____ goals scored by second player

   (#) _____ goals scored by third player

This drill can be varied so that once Player A handballs to B he gets into position to block C, giving B a little more time to score the goal.

Success Goal = To score 10 goals from 10 shots

Your Score = (#) _____ goals

7. Chase and Kick

Play in pairs using markers as a goal. Players stand alongside one of the markers. Player A rolls the ball about 25 metres away. Player B chases after it, gathers, turns and kicks at goal. Player A has given B about 5 metres start and then tries to intercept the shot at goal or to grab hold of B. Have 10 tries each to see who scores the most goals.

Success Goal = To score 8 goals from 10 attempts under pressure

Your Score = (#) _____ goals

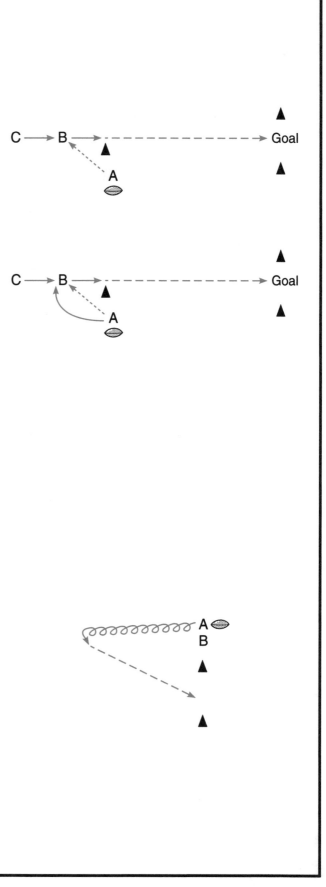

8. Receive and Shoot

Player A runs and kicks the ball between the markers to B who takes the ball, turns and handballs to C who is running past. Player C now kicks to D standing between the markers. Player D handballs to E (A's replacement), etc. Each player follows the ball to the next group. Continue until every player has had 10 kicks to see who kicked the most goals.

Success Goal = 10 goals from 10 shots

Your Score = (#) _____ goals

9. Letter Kick

Four players lettered A, B, C, D are in an area about 50 metres square. All are moving where they like in the square but trying to get well away from the others. Player A has the ball and passes it to B. Player B receives it and passes to C who likewise receives and passes to D who then passes to A, and so on. All players are moving all the time. Continue until all players have kicked the ball 10 times. A successful pass is one that is catchable and is worth 2 points. One point is awarded for each mark. Take off one point if you drop a player's pass.

Success Goal = More than 16 points out of a possible 20

Your Score =

    (#) _____ points scored by you

    (#) _____ points scored by second player

    (#) _____ points scored by third player

    (#) _____ points scored by fourth player

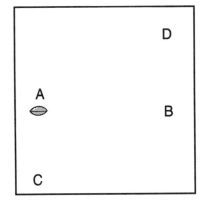

Step 6   Running and Bouncing

As we have seen, Australian football is an aggressive game that relies heavily on attack. One of the ways that a player can attack and set up offensive patterns is to run with the ball. As the rules state:

> A player may hold the ball for any length of time provided he is not held by an opponent. If he runs with the ball he must bounce it or touch the ground with it at least once every 15 metres from the commencement of his run whether he is running in a straight line or turning or dodging.

WHY RUNNING AND BOUNCING SKILLS ARE IMPORTANT

Some coaches discourage running with the ball because it tends to delay delivery of the ball downfield. However, if a player can attack the ball at speed, take possession and then accelerate to run his full distance (and with one bounce he is able to run 30 metres), this gives him balance for disposal and adds distance and speed to the attack. Running can be a tactic to get the ball through or over a line when opponents have a defensive edge through size and/or marking ability. An aggressive runner who will take the ball and challenge opponents to catch him also gains a psychological advantage. Running aggressively and well is a skill and tactic that should be developed. You must take the ball (either by mark or gather) at speed and then accelerate and balance prior to giving a kick or a handball. Good players recognise and understand the advantages of aggressive running and that the player who does not take the ball at speed and then maintain that speed becomes easy prey for defenders. The skill of baulking while running at speed is also important in off-balancing a defender trying to tackle a running player.

Once having run his full distance, the player will need either to dispose of the ball or to bounce it. The run and bounce is an important attacking move that can draw defenders out of position.

Additionally, bouncing the ball is an important skill that should be learned and developed early because of its similarity to the early stages of kicking.

HOW TO RUN AND BOUNCE THE BALL

When running, hold the ball in both hands. From here firmly guide the ball by one hand down to the ground in such a manner that the ball hits on its bottom front third in front of the foot on the same side of the body as your guiding hand. In this manner the ball will come back to you (see Figure 6.1).

As shown in Figure 6.1b, the hand doing the bouncing (and good players are able to use either hand) is more on top of the ball than when you are kicking. In fact, the thumb will be past the lace of the ball, and the tip of the fourth finger will be on the side seam. The fingers are spread and little if any contact is made between the palm of the hand and the ball.

The faster you are moving, the farther in front you will have to bounce the ball so that it comes right back into your hands without slowing your run.

From the very beginning you should learn to bounce the ball with either hand. This will allow you to get an effective lead to kicking with either foot and to bounce the ball on the side farthest from an opponent.

Many players, novice and experienced, make the mistake of bouncing the ball almost immediately upon possession. This is discouraged as it slows the player down. Also, there is always an element of risk in a bounce. Take the ball, accelerate away with it and bounce only after covering 15 metres.

Don't try to bounce when the ground is wet, slippery or muddy. Instead, simply touch the ball onto the ground every 15 metres. Do this by bending at the knees and hips, holding the ball in both hands and touching it to the ground slightly to one side of your body (see Figure 6.2).

Figure 6.1 Keys to Success: *Bouncing the Ball*

Preparation Phase

1. Ball held in two hands ____
2. Bouncing hand more to top of ball ____
3. Fingers control the ball (not palm) ____
4. Elbow bent and close to the side ____

a

b

Execution Phase

1. Ball directed with the top hand ____
2. The ball is bounced by straightening the arm ____
3. The elbow is kept close to the side ____
4. Ball is bounced in-line with the leg on the same side as the guiding hand ____
5. Ball is bounced in advance of the body ____

c

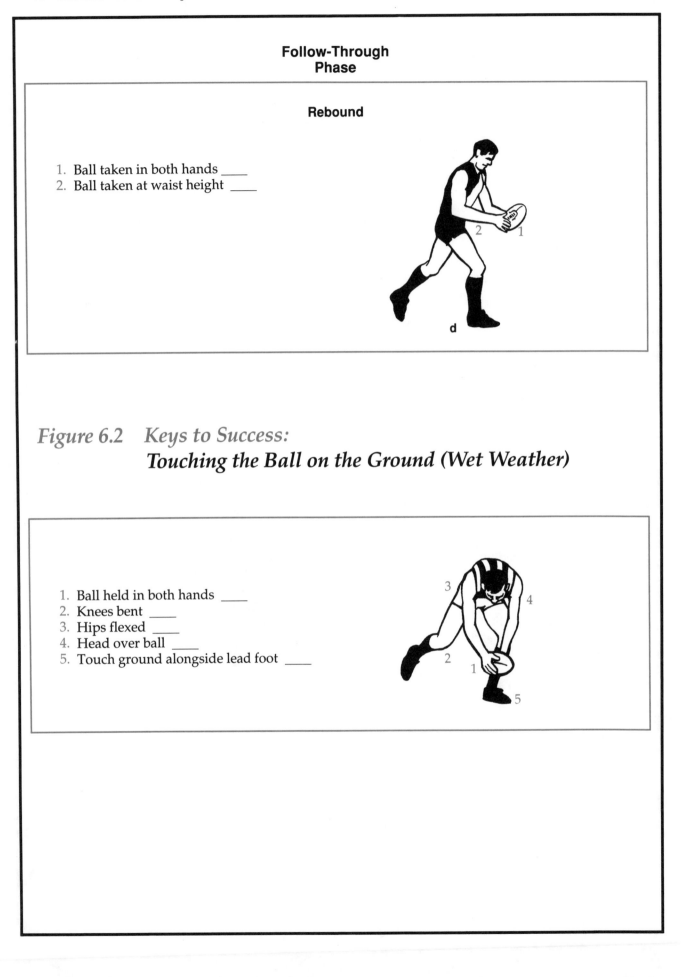

**Follow-Through
Phase**

Rebound

1. Ball taken in both hands ____
2. Ball taken at waist height ____

Figure 6.2   Keys to Success:

Touching the Ball on the Ground (Wet Weather)

1. Ball held in both hands ____
2. Knees bent ____
3. Hips flexed ____
4. Head over ball ____
5. Touch ground alongside lead foot ____

Detecting Errors in Bouncing the Ball

ERROR ⦸	CORRECTION
1. Overrunning the ball.	1. Make sure that you bounce the ball out far enough to allow you time to run into it. The ball needs to be bounced with a definite, firm action. Practise to gain confidence.
2. The player is tackled when bouncing the ball.	2. Accelerate and run 'flat out'. Do not attempt to bounce the ball when it's not necessary. Do not keep possession when you should kick or handball. Teammates should shepherd or warn the runner of the likelihood of the tackle.

Bouncing Drills

1. Stationary Bounce

Bounce the ball while standing still. Practise with both hands separately. If you are practising with a partner, have two or three bounces before handballing the ball to him. Copy your partner. If he does a figure eight around the knees (or some other ball-handling trick) before he bounces, you do the same. If you and a partner both have a ball see if you can bounce at the same speed. Are you able to use your partner as a 'mirror' while bouncing? Face him and bounce at the same speed; if he is bouncing with the right hand, you will need to bounce with your left.

Success Goal = 25 controlled bounces

Your Score = (#) _____ controlled bounces

2. Follow-the-Leader Bounce

With a partner, play follow the leader. Run at various speeds and bounce the ball every 15 metres. Once you have bounced (and caught) the ball, handball it into the air or put it on the ground so that your partner, following behind you, takes possession, runs 15 metres, bounces the ball and hands over possession in a similar fashion. Try also using specific patterns. For example, zig zag, circle or figure eight while bouncing with the appropriate hand.

Success Goal = 5 successful transfers between partners after controlled bouncing

Your Score = (#) _____ successful transfers between partners after controlled bouncing

3. Run the Maze

With a partner, scatter 10 markers at some distance from each other. Your partner then stands between 2 additional markers about 30 metres from the 10th marker. Run hard at the ball on the ground, pick it up and run the maze pattern, bouncing the ball as you pass each marker. Score 1 point for each successful bounce. As you pass the last one, kick the ball to your partner, who then runs.

Success Goal = 10 controlled bounces

Your Score =

(#) _____ controlled bounces by you

(#) _____ controlled bounces by your
        partner

WHY BAULKING, FEINTING AND TURNING ARE IMPORTANT

Part of the aggressive running game is baulking and turning. When you are carrying the ball and are approached by an opponent, do not panic into a hasty disposal. Practise dodging an opponent and placing him out of position for the ensuing play.

Although they can and should be introduced to young players, these skills are regarded as quite advanced. Do not devote a lot of time to them early, however, as mastery may be difficult.

HOW TO EXECUTE THE BLIND TURN

In the blind turn, the player is pursued from behind. The player feints (usually by moving the ball to one side), then uses a strong foot action to push off in the opposite direction, as illustrated in Figure 6.3. If the feint is successful the pursuer follows the first movement and takes himself out of position.

Figure 6.3   *Keys to Success:*
                 Blind Turn

**Preparation
Phase**

The Feint

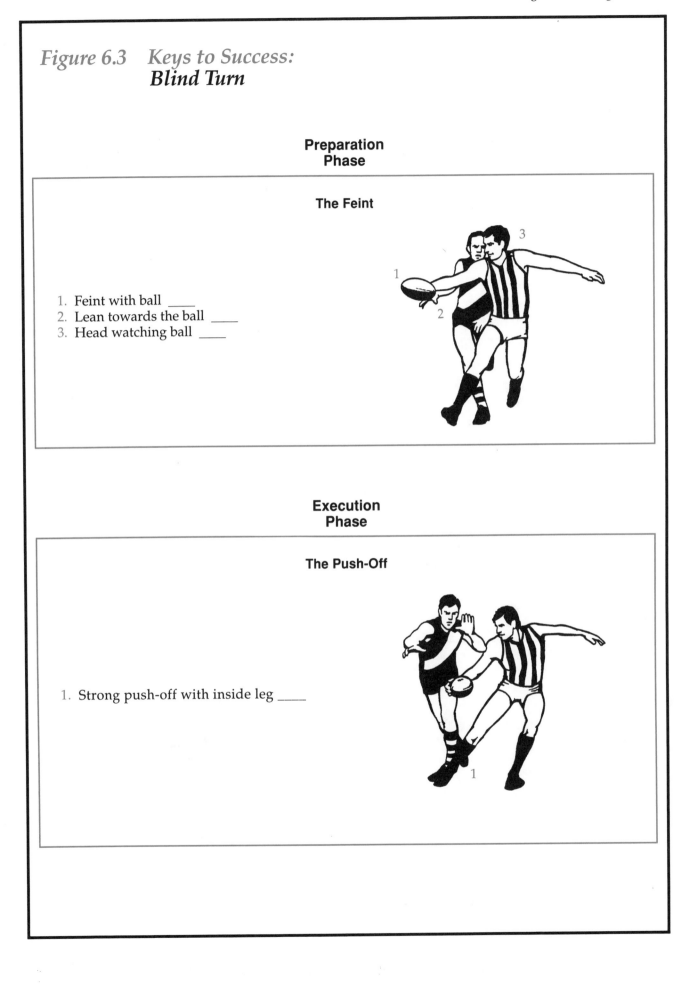

1. Feint with ball ____
2. Lean towards the ball ____
3. Head watching ball ____

**Execution
Phase**

The Push-Off

1. Strong push-off with inside leg ____

**Follow-Through
Phase**

1. Bring the ball close to the body as you turn ____
2. Balance and accelerate away ____

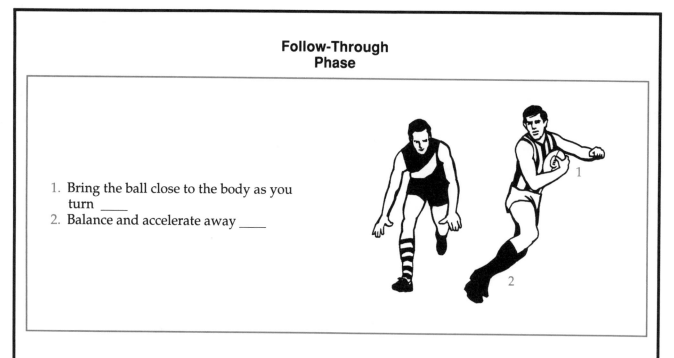

HOW TO EXECUTE THE DOUBLE-BACK

An extension to the blind turn is the double-back, where the ball has not yet been gathered. The leading player baulks in one direction and at the same time knocks the ball back with his hand. He then pivots on his track and gathers the ball while running away from his pursuer (Figure 6.4).

Figure 6.4 *Keys to Success:*
The Double-Back

**Execution
Phase**

1. Bend knees ____
2. Flex at hips ____
3. Knock the ball back behind ____
4. Turn back to recover ball ____

HOW TO EXECUTE THE BAULK

Met from the front, the attacking player has several options. The first is to draw the defender towards him and then handball over the defender's head to a teammate in the clear. But if the attacking player wants to maintain possession he can try to baulk (see Figure 6.5). Here the ball is thrust to one side to give an indication of moving to that side. Then the player pushes off strongly to the other side and swerves past the off-balanced opponent. The baulk is sometimes effectively used to get past a player standing the mark, allowing the player with the ball to 'play on'.

The attacking player's second option is to baulk and pivot. Here as the swerve is made the player pivots away from the opponent.

Figure 6.5   Keys to Success:
Baulk

Preparation Phase

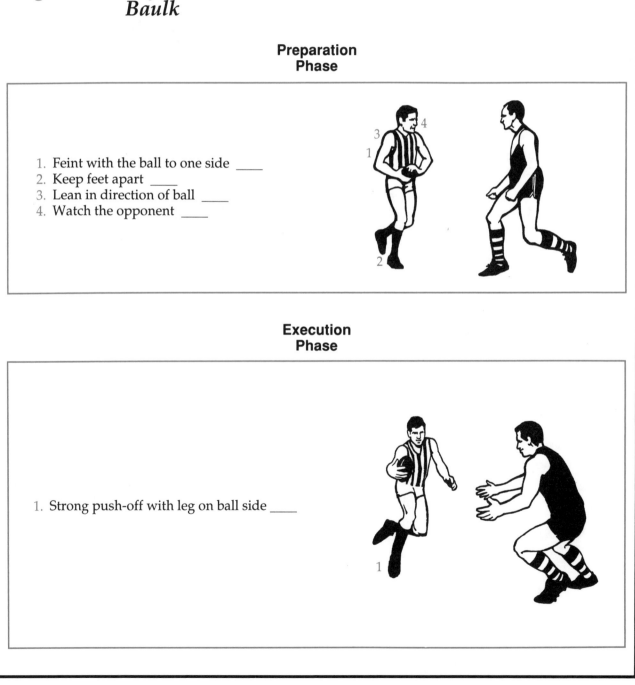

1. Feint with the ball to one side ____
2. Keep feet apart ____
3. Lean in direction of ball ____
4. Watch the opponent ____

Execution Phase

1. Strong push-off with leg on ball side ____

Follow-Through
Phase

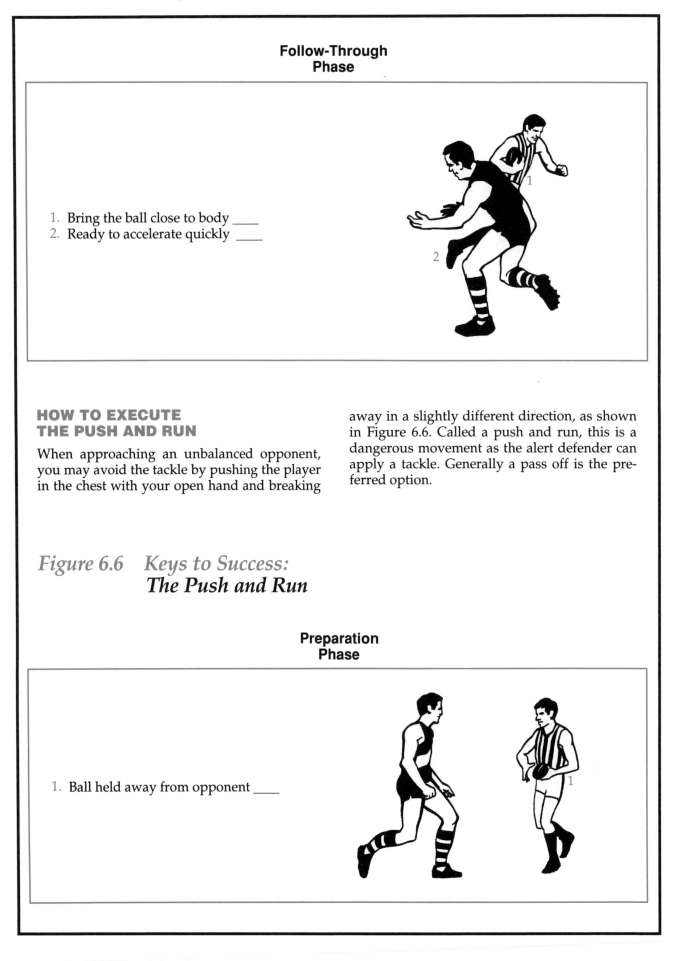

1. Bring the ball close to body ____
2. Ready to accelerate quickly ____

HOW TO EXECUTE THE PUSH AND RUN

When approaching an unbalanced opponent, you may avoid the tackle by pushing the player in the chest with your open hand and breaking away in a slightly different direction, as shown in Figure 6.6. Called a push and run, this is a dangerous movement as the alert defender can apply a tackle. Generally a pass off is the preferred option.

Figure 6.6   Keys to Success:
The Push and Run

Preparation
Phase

1. Ball held away from opponent ____

Execution Phase

1. Ball held away from opponent ____
2. Hand flat on opponent's chest ____
3. Elbow slightly bent ____
4. Strong straightening of the arm ____
5. Push off with the foot closest to opponent ____

Follow-Through Phase

1. Accelerate away from opponent ____

Holding the Ball

It is important to understand the Holding the Ball rule, which states that

A player in possession of the ball and held by an opponent must attempt to dispose of the ball immediately by kicking or handballing.

The spirit of the rule is to allow a player time to dispose of the ball. However, if he is tackled while baulking, feinting or the like, he will have had that time and will need to dispose of the ball *as he is tackled* or else be penalised. Therefore, trying to evade a tackle becomes a risk—particularly if a player habitually tries to avoid or break a tackle rather than dispose of the ball.

Detecting Running, Feinting and Baulking Errors

ERROR ⊘   **CORRECTION**

1. Player is tackled.	1. A player should not be caught if he is running in the open. Safety first dictates that the ball be disposed of by handball or kick before a tackle is likely. When pivoting, make the turn away from the tackling player and not into him. If a tackle is likely, lift your arms so that they will not be caught to allow for a handball.

Some Basic Dodging and Turning Drills

1. Target Dodge

By yourself, run towards a point post. As you get to the post, baulk or pivot and, having cleared it, handball the ball at the goal post. Try this coming from different angles. Have 10 tries and score a point for every hit on the target post.

Success Goal = To score 10 hits from 10 tries

Your Score = (#) _____ hits

2. Partner Dodge

Holding a ball, face your partner. Run towards him, trying to avoid his tackle, and try to hit the target with a handball. Score two points for hitting the target, one for missing and none if you are tackled so that you can't handball. Change over and have 10 tries each.

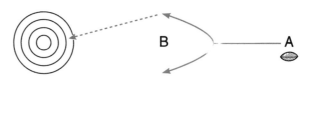

Success Goal = To score more than 15 points from your 10 tries

Your Score = (#) _____ points

3. *Chase and Dodge*

Practice in pairs. One player holds a ball and starts 1 metre in advance of the other. On a signal the two players sprint to a marker 10 metres away, circle it, and run back with the back player trying to catch and tackle the ball carrier. The carrier attempts to hit the target with a handball.

Same scoring as for Partner Dodge.

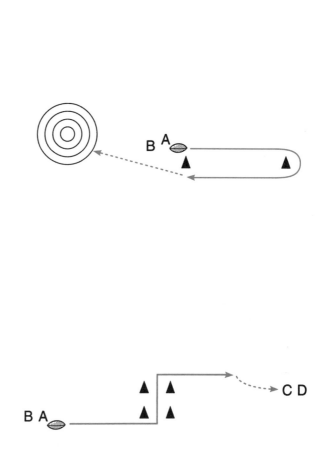

Success Goal = To score more than 15 points from your 10 tries

Your Score = (#) _____ points

4. *Side-Step Relay*

A relay race where the players carry the ball and side-step through the markers as shown.

Success Goal = Your team wins best out of three races

Your Score = (#) _____ of wins for your team

5. *Aggressive Running*

Work with two others, one acting as a starter. Put a ball on the ground 15 metres away. The two contesting stand shoulder to shoulder. On the signal they sprint to the ball and pick it up. A point is awarded to the person getting the ball. A tip: When the signal is given, spread both arms and try and push off your opponent. This exercise can be done around markers, and players try to hold their position as they round each marker.

Success Goal = To get to the ball first on at least three out of five attempts

Your Score = (#) _____ times you reached the ball first

Step 7 Ruckwork

Ruckwork is the contesting of a ball that has been either bounced or thrown up by the umpire. The objective is to tap the ball in the air to a teammate. Ruckwork is done to start the game, to begin each quarter or to restart after each goal. Ruckwork is also done when the umpire wishes to clear a scrimmage or when the ball is disputed with no player having clear possession. Ruckmen compete for the ball from a 'throw in' when a boundary umpire returns the ball into play after it has gone 'out of bounds'.

WHY ARE RUCKWORK SKILLS IMPORTANT?

In junior football, the central umpire can nominate any two players to contest the 'ball up', so every player will need to know and to practise the basic techniques of ruckwork. In senior football, however, ruckwork is the province of the taller, larger players, called *ruckmen*.

The ruckman's objective is to get the disputed ball to a teammate who will be in position either to run away with it or to dispose of it by handball or kick to his team's advantage. This is sometimes called 'getting first use of the ball'. Any player may use the rucking technique to get the ball to advantage if it is bouncing high or if he is not in a position to mark (although usually it is surer to take the bouncing ball in both hands and handball to a teammate).

HOW TO BE SUCCESSFUL AT RUCKING

Figure 7.3 illustrates the important factors in making a success in ruckwork, whether the contest takes place at the centre bounce or at a boundary throw-in.

As with any ball skill, keeping your eyes on the ball is vital. When confronted directly by the opposition ruckman, you may be tempted to look at him rather than at the ball. Resist this temptation and keep your eyes on the ball. Learn and practise the fundamentals of rucking:

• Use both your arms and your legs to get height. Generally, leap off one foot (the foot opposite the hand that is reaching for the ball).

Bend the other leg for lift and to offer protection from body contact. Many ruckmen wear shin guards.

• Time your leap so that you contact the ball as high as possible. Be aware, however, that the ball may not bounce straight up, in which case adjustments in movement and timing need to be made.

• The open hand is more accurate than a closed fist for 'palming' the ball to a waiting teammate. Even greater accuracy is achieved by using your fingertips rather than the flat of your hand.

• Direction is achieved by turning your wrist so that your hand is facing the direction you want the ball to go.

• In trying to hit for distance rather than accuracy (as when trying to clear the ball away from a congested area or defensively through the goals or towards the boundary), punch the ball with a clenched fist in much the same fashion as spoiling a mark.

• Where both ruckmen are approaching the ball from the same direction (as for throw-ins and as is allowed for by the rules for ball ups other than in the centre circle), use the hand closest to your opponent. If possible, use both hands if you are trying to bring the ball down in front of you.

• Make sure that your teammates know where you are trying to hit the ball (see step 12 on team play). They should call to you, and you will need to hit to the vocal target. Your eyes should be on the ball.

There are several approaches to the ball and opponent in ruckwork, and they are illustrated in Figure 7.1. At a centre bounce at the start of each quarter and after each goal the ruckmen must approach each other from either side of the line drawn across the centre circle.

Players will generally approach each other straight on (Figure 7.1a) but this will vary depending on tactics and size. Often a smaller ruckman will try to manoeuvre to enable him to come in from the side of his opponent, much like the tactic used for a boundary throw-in where the players are likely to be side by side (Figure 7.2).

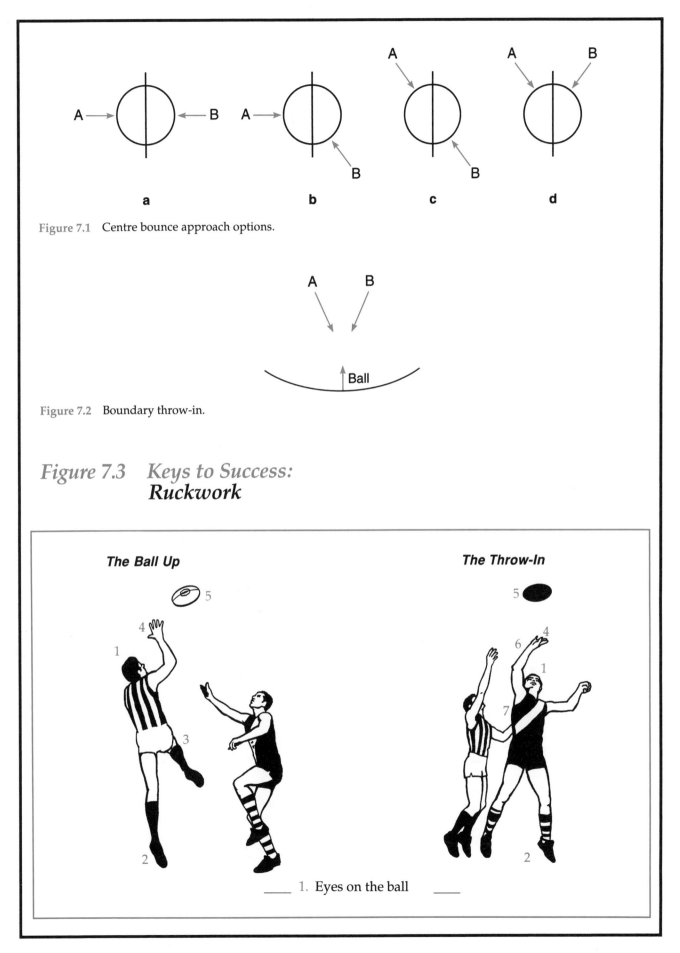

Figure 7.1   Centre bounce approach options.

Figure 7.2   Boundary throw-in.

Figure 7.3   Keys to Success:
Ruckwork

The Ball Up

The Throw-In

_____ 1. Eyes on the ball _____

2. Leap off one foot ____
3. Bend knee of other leg ____

2. Two-foot take-off ____

____ 4. Open hand   ____
____ 5. High ball contact ____

6. Use hand closest to
   opponent ____
7. Body against
   opponent ____

Detecting Rucking Errors

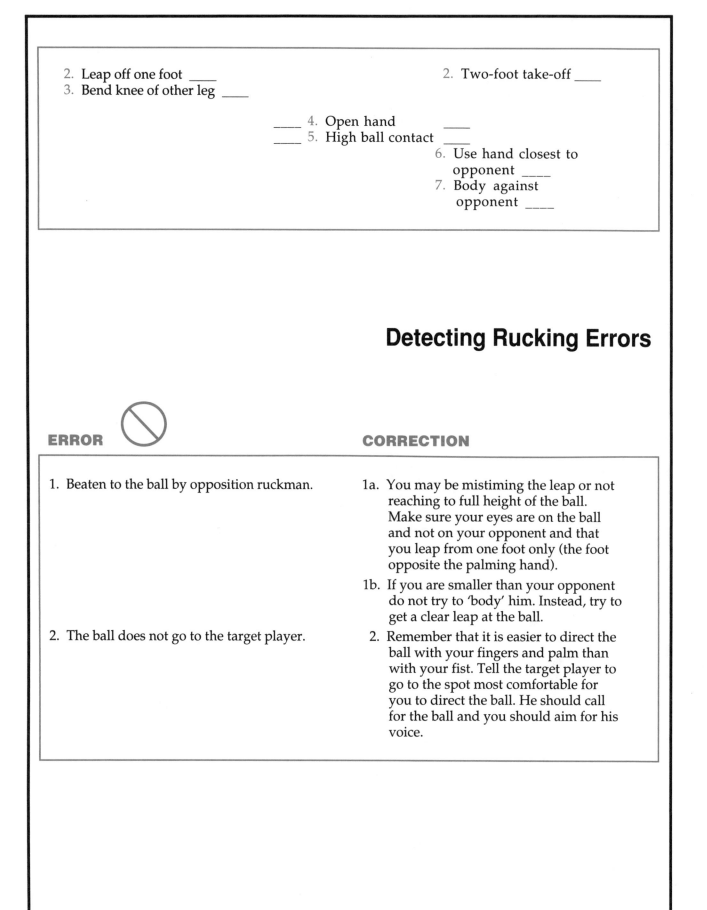

ERROR

CORRECTION

ERROR	CORRECTION
1. Beaten to the ball by opposition ruckman.	1a. You may be mistiming the leap or not reaching to full height of the ball. Make sure your eyes are on the ball and not on your opponent and that you leap from one foot only (the foot opposite the palming hand).
	1b. If you are smaller than your opponent do not try to 'body' him. Instead, try to get a clear leap at the ball.
2. The ball does not go to the target player.	2. Remember that it is easier to direct the ball with your fingers and palm than with your fist. Tell the target player to go to the spot most comfortable for you to direct the ball. He should call for the ball and you should aim for his voice.

Some Ruckwork Drills

1. Target Rucking

By yourself, throw the ball into the air and leap, attempting to palm it to imaginary teammates. Place five markers (hoops or cones) about you and try to direct the ball to them. Number the markers and try to hit each in turn before progressing to the next one.

Success Goal = To hit each target in succession with no misses

Your Score = (#) _____ hits without missing

2. Partner Ruckwork

A partner tosses the ball into the air and you try and hit it back to him. Add difficulty by having your partner toss the ball and then move and call for you to hit the ball to him. Have five turns and change over.

Success Goal = To get the ball back to your partner four out of every five attempts

Your Score = (#) _____ successful attempts

3. Ruck Shootout

Use the numbered targets you used in Target Rucking. The thrower calls out the number of the target you are to try and hit. Have 10 tries and change over. Who scored the most hits out of 10?

Success Goal = To score more hits than your partner

Your Score =
   (#) _____ hits scored by you
   (#) _____ hits scored by your partner

4. *Hit to the Call*

Played with three players. Player A throws the ball into the air and B (the ruckman) tries to hit it back to either A or C who are both calling for the ball. Change over.

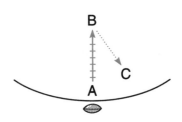

Success Goal = For the ruckman to hit the ball back to A or C 4 out of 5 attempts

Your Score =

(#) _____ out of 5 attempts by you

(#) _____ out of 5 attempts by second player

(#) _____ out of 5 attempts by third player

5. *Competitive Ruckwork*

Play with two partners. Player A throws the ball up for B and C to contest. Both B and C try to get the ball back to A. Change over roles after each contest. Score 1 point for each successful attempt.

Success Goal = Players B and C try to outscore each other

Your Score =

(#) _____ points scored by you

(#) _____ points scored by first opponent

(#) _____ points scored by second opponent

6. *Competitive Ruckwork With Targets*

Same as #5 but this time with a target for each player to try and hit. Have five contests each, changing after each so that you are not competing against the same player all the time. Score 1 point if you win the ruck contest and another 3 points if you hit the target.

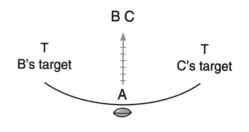

Success Goal = To score more than 10 points

Your Score = (#) _____ points

Part II
Defensive Football Skills

The legendary AFL coach Allan Jeans once stated, 'If your opponents are held scoreless, your team only has to score one point to win—defense *is* important!' Holding a team scoreless is unlikely, but the point is that all players, no matter what their position, must recognise the crucial role of defense. Defensive skills and strategies are fundamental to all game plans. Obviously, some players have greater defensive responsibilities than others. Players in this category are the six players forming the halfback and fullback lines, the *backmen*. They take intense pride in restricting their opponents to as few possessions as possible and minimising their scoring. Their aggression, confidence, attack on the ball and their run are instrumental to mounting counterattacks, often leading to a goal. Similarly, players whose position on the field may be in attack will have to be prepared to employ defense against a possible counterattack by the opposition. No player is only an attacker or a defender; games are lost by players forgetting the defensive aspect of their game. The centre line player who does not come out of attack as quickly as he went in, the forward who does not chase, the rover who does not check, the missed or weak tackle, the lack of discipline to spoil an opponent's mark—these are just a few examples of defensive mistakes that prove costly. Opponents known to have a poor defensive side of their game can be exploited by 'running off' them and mounting a counterattack. Unfortunately, it is custom in the compilation of game statistics to record the *offensive* details—the kicks, marks, handballs and goals scored—and not the *defensive* tackles, blocks off the foot, shepherds, spoils or chases. Headlines and photographs illustrate the match-winning mark and the 'impossible' goal but neglect to give equal billing to the desperate smother, the bone-crunching tackle, the effective shepherd or defensive spoil that may have had as much or even more bearing on the game's result. But the players and coaches recognise the importance of defense. It is not coincidental that many Best Team Man awards go to the players with exceptional defensive skills.

Defensive skills are characterized by commitment, desperation and discipline. So much good defensive work can be attributed to a player's intense desire to stop his opponents from getting the ball, or if they have it, to stop them from making effective use of it. The valued team player may never win any awards from the media, but he is relied upon to tackle, block, shepherd, spoil, chase and do anything in his power to legally deny the opposition possession. A team of 21 such players would be an awesome opponent.

Step 8   Tackling

If a player has possession of the football he may be tackled.

A player in possession of the ball may be tackled and grasped in the area below the top of the shoulders and on or above the knees. The tackle may be from the front, side or behind provided that the tackle from behind does not thrust forward the player with the ball.

WHY IS TACKLING IMPORTANT?

Defenders tackle to stop or at least slow the ball carrier's progress. They hope also to make it difficult for the carrier to dispose of the ball, leading to a free kick for holding the ball. A vigorous tackle may also cause a poor or illegal disposal; this too could lead to a free kick, and it certainly yields a chance for the defensive team to take possession. Tackling is an aggressive skill requiring a determined commitment backed by strong action. Those who half-heartedly tackle are rarely successful, sometimes hurt and usually brushed aside by the opposition.

HOW TO EXECUTE THE TACKLE

In tackling, watch the player's hips and not the ball. A good, agile attacker can use ball movement to deceive a tackler into moving the wrong direction and missing the tackle.

Strive to be as close to the attacker as possible for the tackle. Keep your head and shoulders tucked in against his body. Keep your head up. Do not jump into the tackle—keep both feet on the ground.

A player who knows he is about to be tackled will try and avoid having his arms pinned by the tackle. As the tackler approaches he will lift the ball with both hands high above his head and try to handball quickly off to a teammate (see Figure 8.1). Therefore try to include at least one of the ball carrier's arms (or both, preferably) in the tackle to minimise the chance for effective disposal.

Figure 8.1   Freeing the arms.

Try to push, pull or swing the player away from the ball. A player who is on the ground is an ineffective player. However, remember that the rules penalise pushing in the back and slinging once possession has been lost.

Greater balance is gained from starting the tackle from a slightly crouched position and driving upwards. This upwards movement is likely to take the opponent off his feet.

See Figure 8.2 for a summary of how to tackle well.

Figure 8.2   *Keys to Success:*
            Tackling

**Preparation
Phase**

1. Eyes on opponent's hips ____
2. Arms spread ____
3. Slightly crouched ____

**Execution
Phase**

1. Head in close and held up ____
2. Shoulders and body hard against
   opponent ____
3. Feet on the ground ____
4. Feet apart ____
5. Arms wrapped around opponent ____
6. Arms pinned to the side ____

Detecting Tackling Errors

ERROR ⊘   **CORRECTION**

1. Free kicks to the opponents.

2. The player with the ball is able to break free from the tackle.

3. The tackled player is able to dispose of the ball.

4. The player is able to avoid the tackle.

1. The ball carrier can be tackled only above the knees and below the shoulders when he is in possession of the ball. If the ball is dislodged or legally disposed of, you must discontinue the tackle. If you are tackling from behind, you must not push the carrier forward as this leads to a free kick for 'in the back'. Drop down when making the tackle so that the movement of both players will be *down* rather than forward.

2. Once you have decided to tackle, move strongly and decisively. A tackle made from a distance with only the arms is easily broken. To prevent this, get in close to your opponent, trying to get your head and shoulders close to his body. Keep your head up.

3. Try to pin one or both arms in the tackle and pull or swing the player off balance.

4. This commonly happens when the tackler watches the ball rather than the ball carrier's hips. Whereas ball movement can easily deceive, the hips signal a dodge early. Running directly at the ball carrier commits the tackler and is often easy to avoid. Watch the hips and stop in front of the ball carrier. He then must commit to a dodge, and in doing so he may become indecisive. By 'propping', you are better placed to adjust your move to the attacker's. Once you decide to tackle, do so with a strong effort.

Some Tackling Drills

1. Partner Tackle

Face your partner who stands about 4 metres away. As he runs straight towards you, tackle him. He gets 2 points if he gets past you or 1 point if he doesn't get past but is able to handball towards a target. No points are scored if you catch one or both of his arms in your tackle. Do 5 tackles and then change over.

Success Goal = To keep your partner from scoring

Your Score =

(#) _____ tackles by you

(#) _____ points by your partner

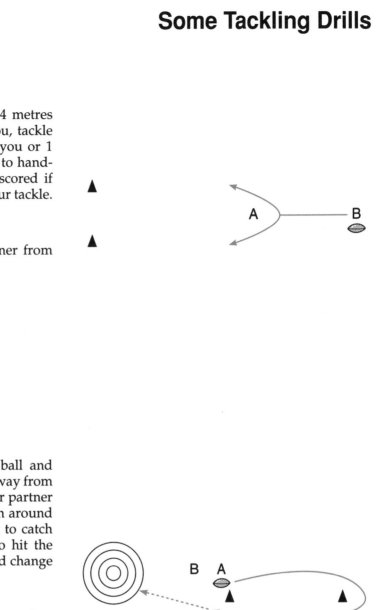

2. Chase and Tackle

Play in pairs. Your partner holds a ball and stands 1 metre in front of you, facing away from a target. On a signal both you and your partner sprint to a marker 10 metres away, run around it, and then run back with you trying to catch and tackle your partner as he tries to hit the target with a handball. Do 5 tackles and change over.

Success Goal = Getting more tackles than your partner

Your Score =

(#) _____ tackles by you

(#) _____ tackles by your partner

3. Reaction Tackle

Play in threes. Players A and B stand facing each other 5 metres apart. Player C rolls or handballs the ball between the players slightly closer to one than the other. The player closest to the ball picks it up and then tries to handball it back to C. The other player tries to prevent this by tackling and pinning the ball carrier's arms. Score 1 point for each successful tackle and pin. Change over after 5 tackles with C taking the place of A or B.

Success Goal = To score more points than your partners

Your Score =

(#) _____ points scored by you

(#) _____ points scored by second partner

(#) _____ points scored by third partner

B

C

A

Step 9 # Bumping, Pushing and Shepherding

The rules of Australian football allow players to be pushed or bumped but there are restrictions as to how and when this can be done.

> A player may be fairly met by an opponent by the use of hip, shoulder, chest, arms or open hands provided he either has the ball or it is not more than five metres away.

However, a free kick will be awarded against a player who pushes, bumps or shepherds an opponent who is in the air attempting to mark.

WHY ARE BUMPING, PUSHING AND SHEPHERDING SKILLS IMPORTANT?

Usually, when a player has possession of the ball you should tackle him. However, there are times when you may be better off bumping the ball carrier instead, such as when he is in the act of kicking or handballing or when he is just out of reach to wrap your arms about him. Your most effective bump or push is made on an unsuspecting opponent or one who is already off-balance. In these cases your bump will knock the ball loose and you or a teammate will likely be able to gather it. If a player does not yet possess the ball and it is being contested, then a bump can be a very effective means of taking the player out of the play.

An alert and effective piece of teamwork is to solidly bump an opponent who is pursuing a teammate (remember that the ball must be within 5 metres at the time). This is a form of *shepherding* and is an important team skill. The player attempts to check or block the approach or tackle of an opponent so that a teammate may take possession of the ball and then dispose of it under less pressure. That is the ultimate objective in shepherding—to take pressure off the teammate.

HOW TO EXECUTE THE BUMP OR PUSH

- Bumping requires an aggressive approach and a well-timed hit.

- As shown in Figure 9.1, you should bunch yourself up by tucking your arm to your side with your elbow close to the hip and by lifting your shoulder to your chin. Bend your knees slightly to get added stability. Deliver the bump with your shoulder, hip or both.

- When attempting to bump, keep both feet on the ground. Otherwise, you might take yourself out of the play along with your opponent.

- You may deliver a bump to the side or front of the player but not to the back or the head nor while he is in the air attempting a mark.

- Push (Figure 9.2) only when you can't get close enough to tackle your opponent or if he is about to dispose of the ball. The push can be to the side or the chest only and must be done with open hands. You need to take care when pushing to the side as this is easily interpreted as a push in the back and a free kick given.

- If the player has the ball it is almost always safer and better to tackle him rather than to push or bump him.

Figure 9.1   **Keys to Success:**
Bumping

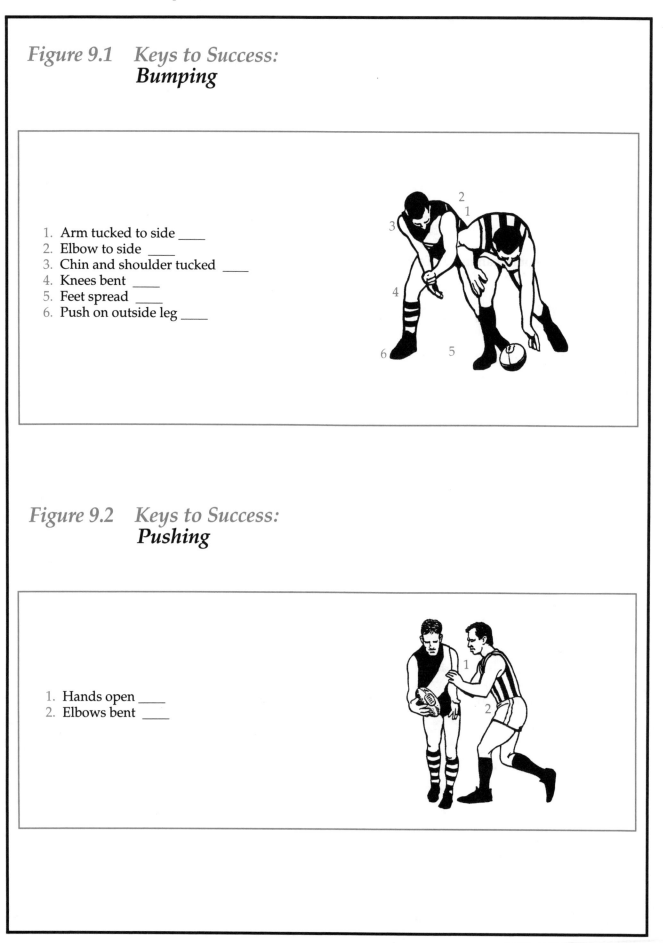

1. Arm tucked to side ____
2. Elbow to side ____
3. Chin and shoulder tucked ____
4. Knees bent ____
5. Feet spread ____
6. Push on outside leg ____

Figure 9.2   **Keys to Success:**
Pushing

1. Hands open ____
2. Elbows bent ____

HOW TO SHEPHERD SUCCESSFULLY

Shepherding can be achieved by bumping but even more common is to position yourself between the attacking opponent and your teammate, thus 'checking' the opponent's movement. Shepherding is even more effective if you spread your arms and stick your rump back into the approaching player (see Figure 9.3).

Move to a position between the opponent and your teammate. As the opponent moves, you move also, always trying to stay between the opponent and your teammate. Talk to your teammate to inform him of pressure and how much time he has to dispose of the ball.

A shepherd, particularly done in a stationary position (as when a teammate is picking up a ball or is about to mark), requires firmness, or the tackler will easily break through. Extend your arms strongly and spread your feet. Always know where your opponent is, either by watching him or feeling his body against yours.

Keep low and lean back into him to hold your ground and not let him brush past you.

Do not hold him in any way, particularly by curling your arms around him, as this will result in a free kick for the opposition as will a shepherd when the ball is more than 5 metres away.

On occasions it is necessary to shepherd the *ball*, rather than a teammate. For instance, when the ball is rolling or going between the goal posts for a goal there is a risk of being tackled and losing the ball if you try to pick it up. You will also shepherd the ball if an opponent is trying to touch it as it goes through the goals (either on the ground or in the air). The principles here are the same as when shepherding a player, but it is probably more important to spread your feet and hold your ground.

During practice it is valuable to work on handballing to a teammate and then running after him with your arms wide out, so that an imaginary opponent would have difficulty getting past you to apply a tackle.

Figure 9.3 **Keys to Success:** *Shepherding*

Preparation Phase

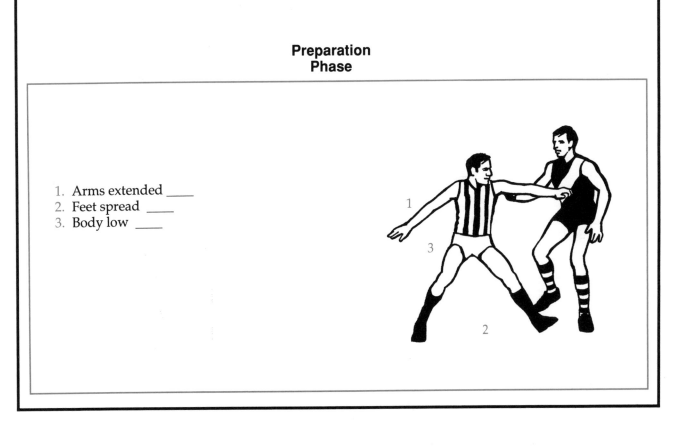

1. Arms extended ＿＿
2. Feet spread ＿＿
3. Body low ＿＿

**Execution
Phase**

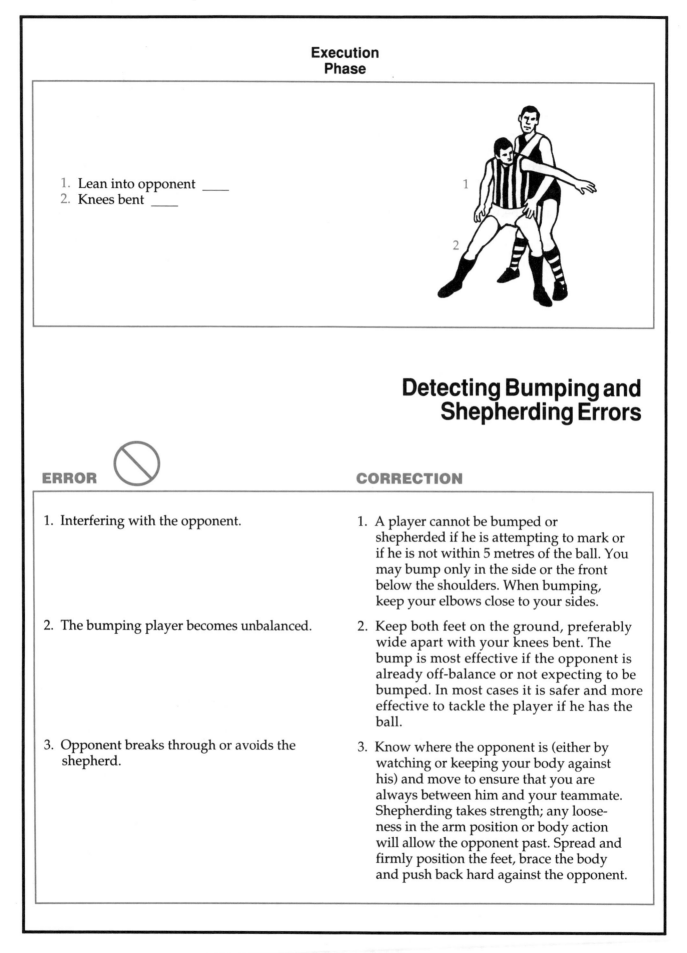

1. Lean into opponent ____
2. Knees bent ____

Detecting Bumping and Shepherding Errors

ERROR   **CORRECTION**

1. Interfering with the opponent.

1. A player cannot be bumped or shepherded if he is attempting to mark or if he is not within 5 metres of the ball. You may bump only in the side or the front below the shoulders. When bumping, keep your elbows close to your sides.

2. The bumping player becomes unbalanced.

2. Keep both feet on the ground, preferably wide apart with your knees bent. The bump is most effective if the opponent is already off-balance or not expecting to be bumped. In most cases it is safer and more effective to tackle the player if he has the ball.

3. Opponent breaks through or avoids the shepherd.

3. Know where the opponent is (either by watching or keeping your body against his) and move to ensure that you are always between him and your teammate. Shepherding takes strength; any looseness in the arm position or body action will allow the opponent past. Spread and firmly position the feet, brace the body and push back hard against the opponent.

Some Basic Tackling, Bumping and Shepherding Drills

Note: Those drills that are used for running and baulking are also worthwhile for tackling and bumping.

1. Protect the Ball

Play with a partner. Put a ball on the ground about 5 metres from both of you. One player protects the ball from the other by shepherding. This drill can be made competitive by having someone time you to see how long you can stop your opponent from touching the ball. Change over. Have two tries each.

Success Goal = To prevent your partner from touching the ball for longer than 30 seconds

Your Score = (#) _____ seconds you kept partner from ball

2. One Versus Three

Requires four players. Three players form a triangle and link hands. Player A has to catch Player B by trying to get around Players C and D who move to bump A and shepherd B. Player A cannot go across the triangle or break the grip. Each have 1 minute to be the chaser.

Success Goal = To keep the protected player from being touched

Your Score = (#) _____ times you let the protected player get touched

3. *Protect the Tail*

Play with four players. Players A, B and C form a line with A facing B and C. Player B puts his hands on A's hips and C holds B's hips. Player D tries to get around A and B to catch C. Player A shepherds. Play for 1 minute, then change over.

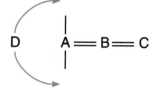

Success Goal = To keep the end player from getting caught when you are shepherding

Your Score = (#) _____ times you allowed the end player to be caught

4. *Protect the Runner*

Players A, B and C stand 1 metre apart. Player A has a ball. On the signal all sprint to the marker with A having to bounce the ball at least once. Player B has to shepherd A by blocking C who is trying to catch A. Vary this by starting with A sitting, B kneeling and C standing. The signal to start can be the ball being handballed to A. Players A, B and C each take 3 turns at shepherding.

C   B   A

Success Goal = To keep the player you are shepherding from getting caught in each of your three tries

Your Score = (#) _____ times you could not stop the tackling player

Step 10 Spoiling and Standing the Mark

When caught behind an opponent with less than an even chance to mark the ball, a player usually elects to *spoil*. In fact a defender will almost always spoil when coming from behind his opponent to contest a ball in the air—it is simply too risky to attempt to outmark from behind. Spoiling is punching the ball away from the opponent with a clenched fist. If the contest is near the opponent's goal the defender will often attempt to punch the ball through the goal conceding one point rather than risk the ball being marked and then kicked for a goal (6 points). When his opponent does mark the ball, a player tries to ensure that his opponent does not play on and has to go back and kick over the spot where the mark was taken, which is a more controlled situation for the defensive team to counter. This is called standing the mark.

WHY IS SPOILING IMPORTANT?

When the ball is in the air, the backman should not risk trying to outmark his opponent—especially in goal-scoring positions. If he is not certain he can take the ball, the defensive player should not attempt to take it. Instead he needs to make it as difficult as possible for his opponent to mark the ball. This is when a spoil is called for and is usually achieved by punching the ball hard. In the forward lines, too, an offensive player out of position will try and bring the ball to ground to his team's advantage. This may mean a spoil to the front of the pack; or if the ball is coming from defense, he may try and punch the ball back over his head in the direction of his goals. In this respect, the spoil can be an effective offensive skill, not merely a defensive one. In all of these situations, players near the spoil need to be aware of the options and take positions where they anticipate the ball will fall.

HOW TO EXECUTE THE SPOIL

The spoil is equally as effective for the high ball and the low. For the low ball you must take care not to interfere with the opponent by reaching over his shoulder or pushing him in the back. Knowing when and how to spoil is part of being a good, disciplined defensive player. The safety-first rule for the defensive player behind in a marking contest is that he must attempt to spoil. Players around him should know this and be ready to gather the ball as it comes to ground. Figure 10.1 illustrates how to spoil correctly.

As with marking, keep your eyes on the ball all the time during the spoil. The spoiling player must time his run and leap to get maximum height before the ball gets to the opponent's hands. Care is taken at all times to avoid interfering with the marking player, particularly by pushing him in the back or reaching or leaning over his shoulder.

Drive your clenched fist through the ball by flexing your arm before extending it as the ball arrives. The arm follows straight through the flight of the ball. This is best done by driving the fist between the marking player's hands and not by swinging the fist in from the side.

The spoiling player's prime objective is to prevent his opponent from marking. However, he should also be conscious of the possible options for the punched ball. He could knock the ball to a teammate. If very near the opponent's goals, he should punch the ball through the goals, conceding a point but saving a possible goal. As a general rule, the ball should be punched towards the boundary rather than into the midline of the field where it is more easily recovered and scored from by opponents. An exception is an opponent's kickoff from a behind—here forwards will try to punch the ball back in the direction of their goals.

While spoiling is a defensive action, the spoiling player can take offensive advantage in that he knows the probable fall of the ball. He can follow up his strong action in the air by an equally strong attack on the ground to turn defense into attack.

Often a player cannot decide whether to jump and spoil because of the presence of teammates competing for the ball. In most cases, if a forward is leaping for a mark his opponent should leap with him and attempt to spoil. This is particularly so for the backman whose opponent has a good run at the pack and a likely 'ride'. The backman has to go with his opponent and attempt to spoil regardless of who is in front.

A skilled forward will attack the ball as if he expects to mark it. To counter this, the spoiling player must be fully committed and make a strong and hard punch. A half-hearted spoil attempt rarely succeeds.

Punching the ball should be the objective in spoiling. However, it is completely within the rules to knock away the arms of the marking player, and this should be done if you cannot reach the ball. This is not nearly as effective as spoiling the ball and can lead to a free kick if done incorrectly, so knocking the hands should only be done as a last defensive possibility.

Figure 10.1   Keys to Success: The Spoil

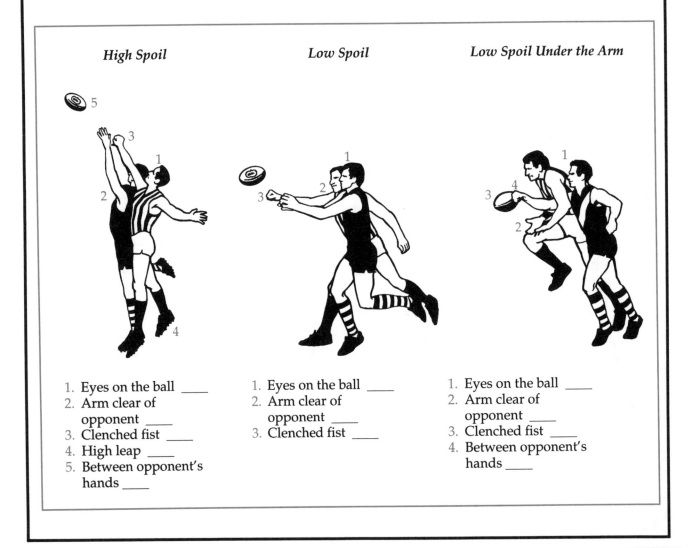

High Spoil

1. Eyes on the ball ____
2. Arm clear of opponent ____
3. Clenched fist ____
4. High leap ____
5. Between opponent's hands ____

Low Spoil

1. Eyes on the ball ____
2. Arm clear of opponent ____
3. Clenched fist ____

Low Spoil Under the Arm

1. Eyes on the ball ____
2. Arm clear of opponent ____
3. Clenched fist ____
4. Between opponent's hands ____

Detecting Spoiling Errors

ERROR   🚫   **CORRECTION**

1. Being outmarked by an opponent.

2. Failure to contact the ball.

3. Interfering with the opponent.

1. For a defender, safety first is the key. If the forward has front position, he will likely mark the ball. Take the initiative and spoil, then try to follow up the loose ball to punch towards teammates or just to prevent the mark. It is almost a golden rule for defenders to never try to mark from behind.

2. This is usually caused by poor timing of the leap and the punch. Drive your fist between the marker's hands rather than swinging from the side across the line of flight of the ball. Keep your eyes on the ball and hit through it. If the ball is not dislodged on contact it may be because your arm is not firmly and vigorously extended.

3. Time your leap. Do not put your hands on the back or shoulders of the front player to try to get height. Do not reach over his shoulders with either arm; spoil by punching between his hands. When spoiling an attempted chest mark, spoil under the marking player's arm to eliminate the possibility of being 'over the shoulder'.

Spoiling Drills

1. Punch Ball

Hold the ball high above and in front of your head with one hand and practise the punching action of spoiling. Practise near the point post and try to punch the ball over the top of the post. Score 1 point if you do. Have 10 tries alternating hands. Are you able to score as many with your left hand as with your right? Are you able to get to the top of the goal post?

Success Goal = 10 spoils to the height of the point post

Your Score =

(#) _____ successful right-hand spoils

(#) _____ successful left-hand spoils

Try a similar exercise but this time hold the ball at different angles to represent the spoil from chest marks. You could do this at the kickoff line and try to get the ball over the goal line. Alternate hands.

Success Goal = 10 spoils to the goal line

Your Score =

(#) _____ right-hand spoils to the goal line

(#) _____ left-hand spoils to the goal line

2. Partner Punch

Do the same drills but have a partner hold the ball for you so that you can jump and punch the ball. Use a similar scoring system to compete with your partner.

Success Goal =

a. 10 spoils to the height of the point post

b. 10 spoils to the goal line

Your Score =

a. (#) _____ spoils to the height of the point post by you

(#) _____ spoils to the height of the point post by your partner

b. (#) _____ spoils to the goal line by you

(#) _____ spoils to the goal line by your partner

3. Leap and Spoil

Play in threes. Player A stands in front of the other two and throws the ball high into the air. The other two compete, with one being the designated marker and the other the spoiler. Have five tries each at marking and spoiling. Players get 2 points for every spoil but lose 1 point each time their opponent marks the ball. Lose 2 points for each free kick awarded by the throwing player against the spoiler for 'over the shoulder' or 'in the back .

Success Goal = To score at least 8 points

Your Score =

(#) _____ points scored by you

(#) _____ points scored by your partner

4. Chest Mark Spoil

Play the same as Leap and Spoil, but this time the ball is thrown at the chest of the leading player with the other trying to spoil. Use the same scoring system.

Success Goal = To score at least 8 points

Your Score =

(#) _____ points scored by you

(#) _____ points scored by your partner

5. End-to-End Spoil

Practise in pairs in end-to-end kicking with the player being caught behind attempting to spoil. Each spoil earns 1 point.

Success Goal = To score more points than your partner

Your Score =

(#) _____ points scored by you

(#) _____ points scored by your partner

6. Team Spoil

In groups of six, work together in two teams of three. Two are at one end acting as spoiler and 'crumber'. (The player who positions himself to gather the falling ball is often described as gathering crumbs.) The third man is 25 to 30 metres away and acts as kicker and marker. Your opponents do the same. The ball is kicked high and two players contest the mark and spoil with the spoiling player trying to get the ball to his teammate on the ground. Talk to your teammate to decide where he is going to try and spoil the ball. Teams score 2 points when they recover the ball but lose 1 when their opponents mark the ball. Rotate the positions after every five kicks to your team.

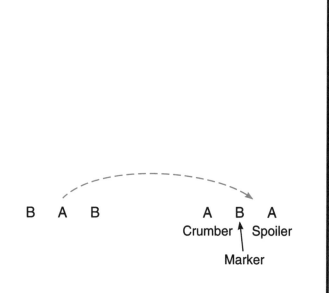

Success Goal = To outscore your opponents

Your Score =

(#) _____ points scored by your team

(#) _____ points scored by your opponents

WHY ARE GUARDING AND STANDING THE MARK IMPORTANT?

Regardless of how well a player is defended, opponents will still mark the ball during the game. At other times a free kick will be awarded. When this occurs, the defending player's aim is to prevent his opponent from playing on and by doing so give his teammates down the field time to cover their opponents. Standing the mark is a vital defensive skill that must be done well or else a 50-metre penalty could be imposed.

When a player has been awarded a mark or a free kick and an opponent unduly holds or deprives him or refuses him possession of the ball, deliberately encroaches over the mark or in any way deliberately delays the play, the spot where the mark or free kick was awarded shall be advanced not more than 50 metres nearer the goal that the player of the team entitled to the kick is attacking.

HOW TO GUARD AND STAND THE MARK

When guarding the mark, hold the player momentarily to prevent him from playing on as the mark is taken or a free kick given. If possible, place one hand on top of the ball, but it must not be held, knocked or punched away (see Figure 10.2). While standing the mark, spread your arms and take a wide stance to make it more difficult for the player with the ball to play on around you (see Figure 10.3). Watch him because he will try to run around you if he can. Practise the following fundamentals of standing the mark:

• On the umpire's whistle, take the position at the spot designated by the umpire and put both hands in the air so that the player has to go back and kick over them. Do not take your eyes off the player.

• If the opponent starts to move to either side, you go to that side also and be ready for the umpire's call of 'play on', at which time you can come forward and attempt to tackle.

• If for any reason a 50-metre penalty is awarded, move back quickly, running backwards and keeping your eyes on the advancing player. He will not be allowed to play on until you are on the mark, but then be ready.

• A ruckman, rover or a follower should not have to stand the mark or a free kick. The ruckman needs to be at the fall of the ensuing kick to fill up the space and to contest the mark;

the others need to be free to follow their opponents into defense. Position players should come up from behind to stand the mark.

• When there is a shot at goal a tall player should stand the mark. He should have his arms extended up and should jump to try to block or touch the ball in flight. At the same time, another tall player (usually a ruckman) should run to the goal line to try and touch the ball as it goes through the goals or to compete in the air if the ball drops short.

Figure 10.2   *Keys to Success:*
Guarding the Mark

1. Briefly hold player ____
2. Guard the ball ____
3. Eyes on the ball ____

Figure 10.3   Keys to Success:
Standing the Mark

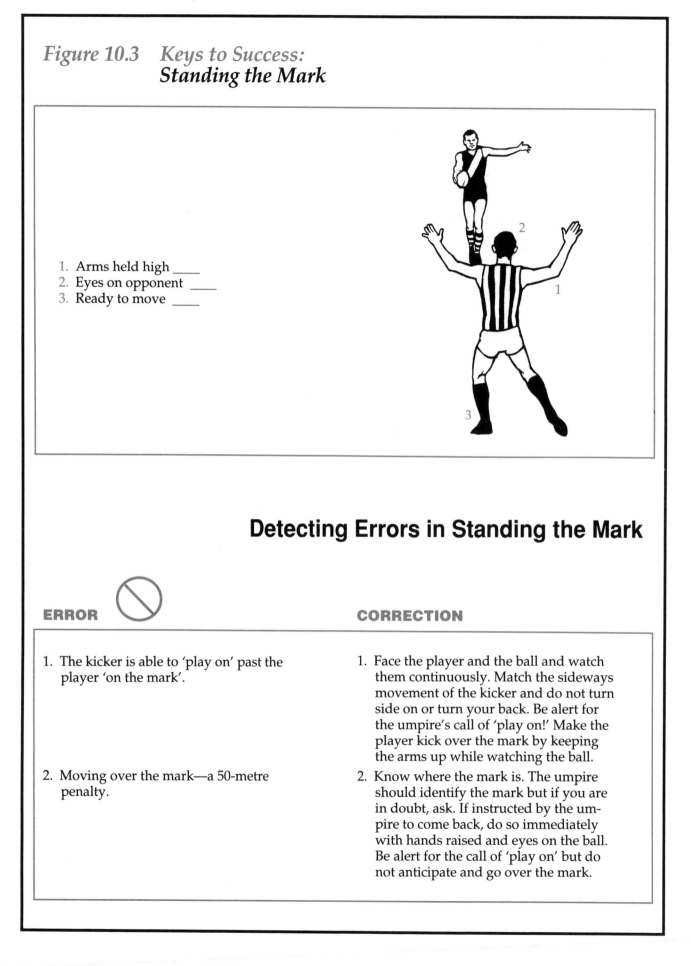

1. Arms held high ____
2. Eyes on opponent ____
3. Ready to move ____

Detecting Errors in Standing the Mark

ERROR   **CORRECTION**

1. The kicker is able to 'play on' past the player 'on the mark'.

2. Moving over the mark—a 50-metre penalty.

1. Face the player and the ball and watch them continuously. Match the sideways movement of the kicker and do not turn side on or turn your back. Be alert for the umpire's call of 'play on!' Make the player kick over the mark by keeping the arms up while watching the ball.

2. Know where the mark is. The umpire should identify the mark but if you are in doubt, ask. If instructed by the umpire to come back, do so immediately with hands raised and eyes on the ball. Be alert for the call of 'play on' but do not anticipate and go over the mark.

Standing the Mark Drills

1. Kick Over the Mark

Play in pairs. Place 10 markers at various distances and angles from the goal. Each player will have one shot at goal from each of the markers. Player A takes the first kick. Player B stands the mark (at the first marker) with hands in the air. Player A kicks at goal over Player B and gets 6 points for a goal and 1 point for a behind. Player B immediately sprints after the ball, recovers it and kicks it to Player A who has moved up to the marker. Player B runs back past A who handballs to B. Player B now takes his kick for goal over A standing the mark. Player A recovers the ball and passes it back to B who has moved to the second marker, and so on.

Success Goal = To score more points than your partner. Try to block or touch the ball that your partner kicks.

Your Score =

(#) _____ points scored by you

(#) _____ points scored by your partner

2. Stand the Mark

Play in threes. Player A kicks the ball to B and C. Player B allows C to mark and then stands the mark, trying to prevent C from playing on and kicking the ball back to A. Player B makes C go back and kick over his mark to A. Change over after 5 kicks.

Success Goal = To prevent your opponent from playing on with a kick

Your Score = (#) _____ times that you allow your opponent to play on with a kick

3. Prevent the Play On

Play the same way as Stand the Mark but this time after kicking, Player A runs up to try and receive a handball from C. Player B tries to prevent the handball. Change roles after each kick.

Success Goal = To prevent your opponent from playing on with a handball

Your Score = (#) _____ times that you allow your opponent to play on with a handball

Step 11 **Smothering**

Often taken as a measure of a player's desperation, the smother is an attempt to block the ball off the foot of an opponent in the act of kicking. A smother is usually attempted when the defensive player is out of position to attempt a tackle or bump and therefore tries to nullify the kick. Although smothering appears difficult and dangerous, if properly executed it is very effective and has minimal risk to the smotherer. Indecision is the main cause of problems in attempting to smother.

WHY IS SMOTHERING IMPORTANT?

This important defensive skill can save goals and even games. Denying your opponents a disposal of the ball, often in a clear position of advantage, is clearly a key play. It may cause a quick turnover of the ball if you can catch opposition players (who had been ready to receive the ball) out of position to defend. In such a case, a 'desperate' defensive measure turns defense into attack.

HOW TO EXECUTE THE SMOTHER

In smothering, timing is vital in that your hands must be over the ball at the right time. It is here that indecision will lead to late positioning.

The smother is generally made from the side or the front with the fingers spread and the thumbs close together or overlapping. The arms are close together and stretched but relaxed so that the impact of the kicked ball can be absorbed.

To smother, position yourself close to the player; your hands are placed in the anticipated path of the ball as it leaves the player's foot. Your palms face the ball. The closer to the foot the smother is made, the better and safer it will be. Your arms protect your face and stop the free swing of the kicker's leg. Keep your eyes on the ball and your head down. Figure 11.1 illustrates the important skills of the smother.

A handball can also be smothered. Here a ball in the hand is the target instead of the ball being kicked. The same principles apply.

Figure 11.1   Keys to Success: *Smothering the Ball*

Preparation and Execution Phases

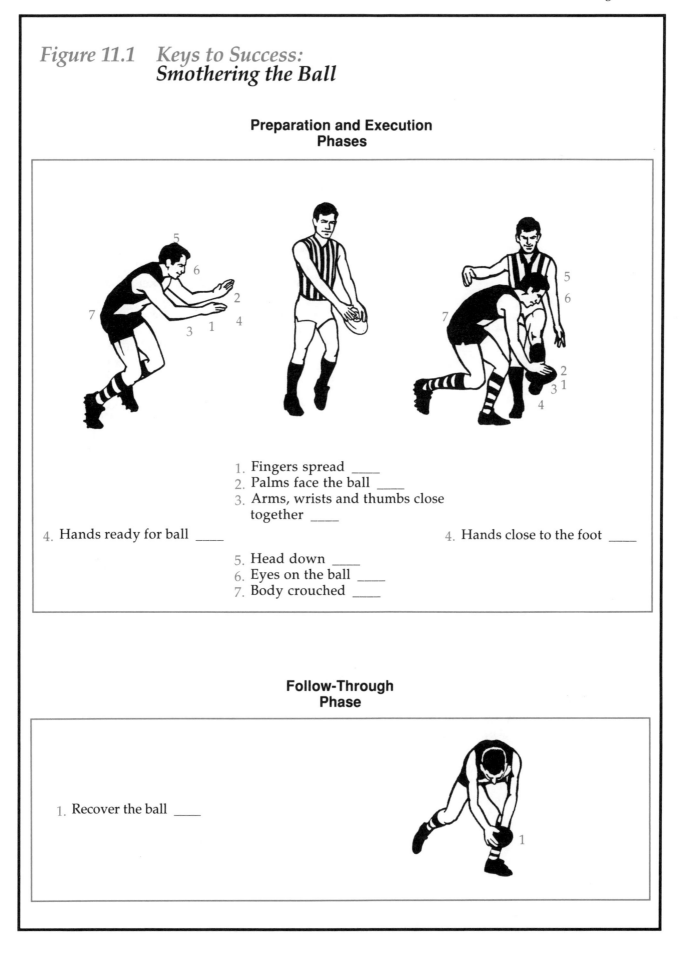

1. Fingers spread ____
2. Palms face the ball ____
3. Arms, wrists and thumbs close together ____

4. Hands ready for ball ____

4. Hands close to the foot ____

5. Head down ____
6. Eyes on the ball ____
7. Body crouched ____

Follow-Through Phase

1. Recover the ball ____

Detecting Errors in Smothering the Ball

ERROR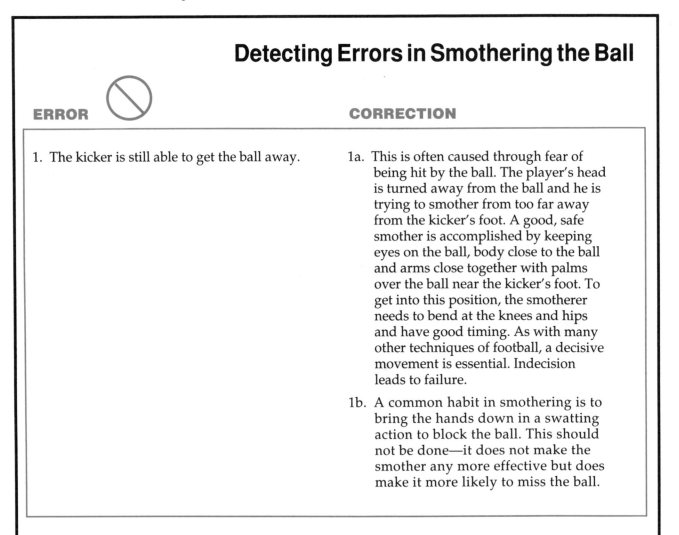

CORRECTION

ERROR	CORRECTION
1. The kicker is still able to get the ball away.	1a. This is often caused through fear of being hit by the ball. The player's head is turned away from the ball and he is trying to smother from too far away from the kicker's foot. A good, safe smother is accomplished by keeping eyes on the ball, body close to the ball and arms close together with palms over the ball near the kicker's foot. To get into this position, the smotherer needs to bend at the knees and hips and have good timing. As with many other techniques of football, a decisive movement is essential. Indecision leads to failure.
	1b. A common habit in smothering is to bring the hands down in a swatting action to block the ball. This should not be done—it does not make the smother any more effective but does make it more likely to miss the ball.

A Smothering Drill

Note: A good exercise is to try such competitive drills as keep-the-ball-away, two on two, or handball football, where tackling is not allowed but smothering is.

1. The Smother

The smother can be practised by Player A handpassing the ball to B, who moves in to kick while C comes from the side to attempt to smother. The angle of C's approach should vary. This exercise should be done first with the kicker stationary and then with the kicker moving to take the ball and kick. Change positions after each kick and have five attempts each to smother the kick from a stationary player and five from a moving player.

Success Goal = To smother all 10 kicks

Your Score = (#) _____ smothers

Part III
Strategy Skills

Many Australian footballers have developed good technique in the basic facets of the game. They take the ball cleanly, kick long and accurately and bump and tackle well. These players may also possess the agility, quickness, strength and endurance that the game requires. But good technique and skills alone have not enabled these players to become good or even average footballers.

Australian football, like many other sports, requires its players to have the ability to use their skills in *game* situations. They need to know which actions are appropriate under changing circumstances, how to allow for different environmental conditions, how to counter different opponents, how to perform automatically under game pressure, how to 'read the play' and be in the right place at the right time and how to make things easier for their teammates. That is, the good footballer needs to *know* the game and possess 'game skills'.

A good player must understand that he cannot practise and perform in isolation and that he needs to learn more than just the skills of handballing, kicking, tackling, etc. A good player also knows the requirements of the game and the basic strategies and tactics that lead to success. Once players have achieved a certain level of skill, their coaches will spend much of practice time employing these skills in team-oriented drills to develop patterns of play. These patterns will not only make the skills of the game automatic for a player but will also help him quickly decide what course of action to take in the variety of situations he is likely to confront in a game.

So, this section of the book concerns some of the basic components of 'game flow'—what a team is trying to achieve in a game and how it goes about it. This will include looking at the different positions on the ground and their particular requirements, going over some team patterns and strategies and reviewing the main rules of the game.

But team play is more than tactics, strategies and rules. It is an old but true saying that a good *team* will usually beat a group of talented individuals. So, we'll also discuss the qualities a good team man possesses, our objective being to make you a more effective player overall.

Step 12 Team Play Skills and the Basic Game Plan

Teams do not win games merely by getting possession of the ball. Nor does the team with the most scoring shots necessarily win. Effective use has to be made of the ball once it is gained. A team may have more marks, kicks and handballs than its opponent yet still be beaten because its tactics and skills have not put those possessions and disposals to advantage.

WHY ARE TEAM PLAY SKILLS IMPORTANT?

Manuals on football play and coaching often show maps of ovals with areas shaded to designate coverage by particular players. Figure 12.1 shows an example.

As I pointed out earlier, Australian football has evolved to the stage where these positional

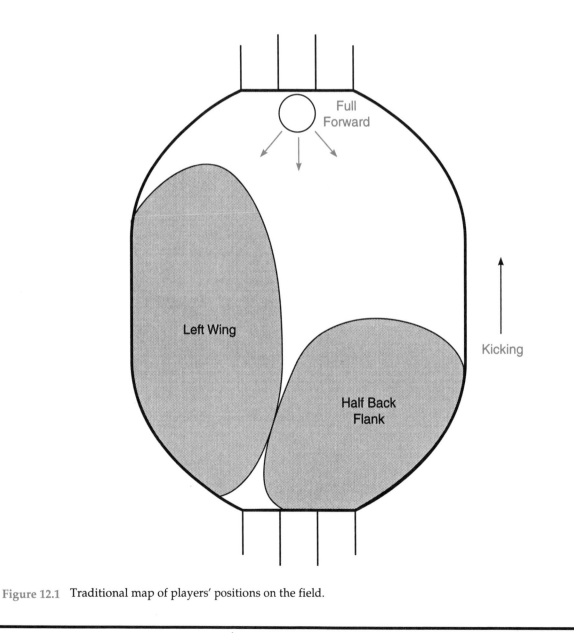

Figure 12.1   Traditional map of players' positions on the field.

concepts are no longer appropriate. Defenders are no longer restricted to following their opponents in particular zones on the field. Today's game demands flexibility in roles, roles that include covering a zone, filling a space, blocking a team's strength, roaming the whole field, making rapid use of interchange players, playing man on man, maximising particular strengths and many more. For example, whereas a wingman not too long ago knew almost precisely where to play, today's wingman can be expected, depending on team plans and strategies, to cover the whole ground from full forward to full back to full forward and on both sides of the ground. It is not unusual to see all four wingmen on the one side of the oval, a half

forward starting behind the centre square and a forward pocket stationed on the wing. The lack of any semblance of a formal offside rule makes this possible. Teams are still named in positions, but contemporary coaches assign different roles to different players of particular positions, not only from match to match but also within a single game. Nevertheless, it is still helpful for all players to identify in general terms their possible roles when named in a position.

FIELD POSITIONS

Figure 12.2 shows names and positions of the 18 players. The major roles of the players are described in the following section.

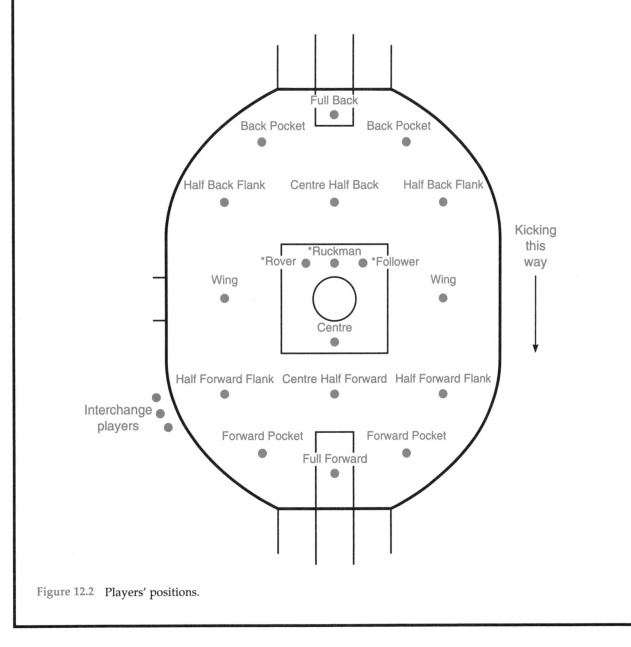

Figure 12.2   Players' positions.

Full Back Line

The full back and the two back pockets make up the full back line. These players' fundamental role is to prevent opponents from gaining possession of the ball and kicking goals. They also try to keep their opponents from using the attacking zone in front of the goals. A full back's performance is ultimately judged by how many goals the opposing full forward kicks. The backs try to spoil their opponents' attempts to mark, and they defend to deny possession of the ball to the forwards. If the defensive players have the ball they become running attacking players, moving the ball out of defense into attack. The back pockets, while being responsible for restricting possession of the ball by their immediate opponents, assist the full back in denying space and the ball to the full forward, who is the likely focal point for opposition attacks.

Half Back Line

The two half back flanks and the centre half back are the line of first defense, but they also are an important group for taking possession of the ball and mounting an attack. A successful team has a half back unit that is dependable in defense but can also carry the ball forward in attack and often kick goals. Effective half back players are always prepared to run past centre and half forward teammates to receive a handball or to offer support. They then get back quickly to their immediate opponents and defend.

The Centre Line

The centre line includes the two wingmen and the centre player. These three are usually good ball-getting, running players who will help turn defense into attack and set up attacking plays. Their main role is to get the ball to forward players, so they are sometimes called 'link' men. These positions are usually manned by very skilled players able to handball with either hand and kick with either foot. They will have good turning agility, an above average ability to 'read the play', a high level of fitness and exceptional team skills.

A basic but essential team discipline is that when your opponents have the ball, you defend, and when your team has the ball, you attack. This is especially important for centre line players, who constantly change from attacking to defending and back again. When their team has possession of the ball, the centre line players run to position themselves to receive and relay the ball. Conversely, once the ball has been 'turned over' to their opponents, the centre line players' first objective is to find and defend strongly against their direct opponents.

As they will run past half forward players to receive a handball or take the ball 'off hands' and have a shot at goal, centre line players often kick goals. In senior football, as centre line players run towards or beyond the 50-metre line they will have a shot at goal. Outside that range they tend to pass the ball to full forward players.

On kickoffs by the opposition, centre line players tend to play behind the players contesting for the mark to be in position to play either a defensive or attacking role depending on which team takes possession of the ball or if the ball runs loose over the back of the pack.

Half Forward Line

The half forward line is made up of the centre half forward and the two half forward flankers. The centre half forward is usually a tall player who becomes the focal point for attacks out of the backline as the ball is brought into the attacking zone. Therefore the centre half forward should be able to mark well overhead. The flankers are generally quick players able to take the ball falling from contested marks and kick accurately for goal on the run. These positions are considered difficult to play—not only are they strongly defended but they require the player to take the ball and then turn towards his goal (unlike other positions that attack the ball straight on and keep going in that direction). Half forwards should work together and not contest marks against each other.

Strong defense is required by half forwards to prevent their opponents from getting the ball and initiating attacking moves. That is, half forwards need to be able to chase and to tackle hard.

Full Forward Line

The full forward and the two forward pocket players make up the full forward line. These are the main goal-scoring players. The full forward is generally a fast leading player to whom teammates will try and kick the ball so that it can be marked and followed by a shot at goal. However, as the ball is often delivered to the area under pressure (and therefore not always accurately), the full forward is also expected to take hotly contested marks and to gather the ball from the ground under pressure. A high marking full forward who can't or won't contest strongly on the ground will be of limited use to his team.

The pocket players are usually of two types: one tall, the other small. The tall pocket player moves behind the full forward when he leads and becomes a second target for the attacking team. This player should be able to mark well overhead and kick accurately for goal. The small pocket player's major role is to position himself to gather the ball falling from the marking contests of the larger forwards and their opponents. Once he has gathered it, he shoots for goal. This player must have speed, agility, good ball and goal sense and accurate goal shooting.

As with the half forwards, the full forward line has a vital role in preventing opponents from mounting an attacking move from deep in the forward line. As soon as the opposition has the ball, the forwards must become desperate, ruthless defenders and fight to hold the ball in their area. A forward who will not chase is a liability to his team.

The Ruckman

As the largest player on the team, the ruckman has both attacking and defensive roles, particularly when the ball is in the air. He is a focal point for many attacking kicks out of defense but will also position himself to try to intercept kicks by the opposition. (Both of these roles come into play when the ball is kicked off following a behind being scored.) To succeed, the ruckman needs to read the play very well. One of his fundamental roles is to position himself near the opposing team's centre half forward to contest marks and in front of the full forward to deny him space into which to lead. He should also be in position to contest marks with the full forward and the larger of the forward pockets.

The Ruck Rover and Rover

The ruck rover and the rover roam the field and initiate many attacking moves. They cover opponents' attacking players, provide additional coverage all over the field and are important links in establishing attacking moves. These players will have exceptional ball-getting and disposal skills. They will be able to read the play and get to where the ball is. Their play is characterised by fearless winning of the ball, tackling and a willingness to run for the entire game. Although primarily attacking players, they defend as well, covering their counterparts when the opposition has the ball.

Interchange Players

Each team is allowed to start three interchange players. These are versatile players who play a variety of positions. Players are freely interchangeable during the game as long as the interchanges occur at the designated part of the field and the interchange official is notified.

WHY ARE BASIC GAME PLAN STRATEGIES IMPORTANT?

Australian football is very much a player-on-player game, but the concept of zones is apparent in game tactics—not so much zones for players, because now some players are encouraged to roam much of the field, but zones of play. Figure 12.3 shows the scoring (attacking) and defensive zones. In kicking for goal the optimal position is from directly in front, so a team wishing to maximise its offensive efforts attempts to get the ball into this position as often as possible. Conversely, the defensive team works to keep the ball out of this area. These two simplistic statements are a generalisation of the main strategies of Australian football—all more sophisticated tactics are built on that foundation.

In general terms, then, a team's basic game plan is to get the ball into its scoring zone and shoot for goal and to deny the opposition from so doing by keeping it to the defensive flanks.

IN DEFENSE

• Apart from trying to gain possession of the ball, the fundamental aim of the defense is to force the opponent into a position that minimises the effectiveness of its possession.

• When kicking out from a point or in general play, back players will rarely kick straight down the field from deep in defense. Instead they will kick to players who have led from the opponent's scoring zone into the defensive flanks.

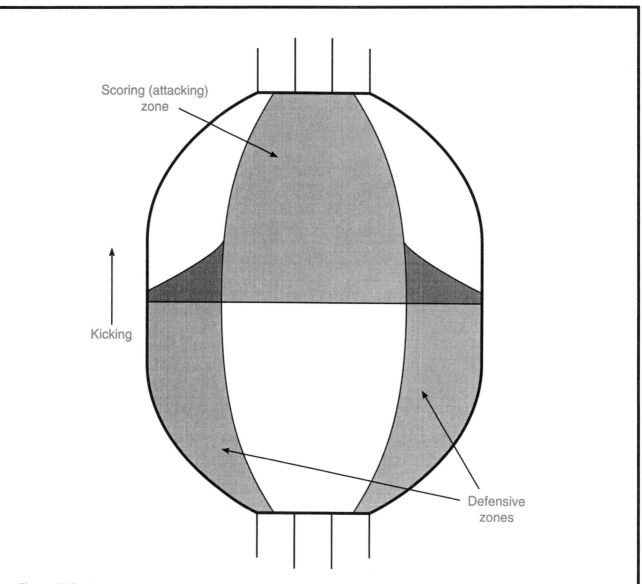

Figure 12.3   Zones of play.

• Rather than turning back and kicking into the middle of the field, players in the back lines will try to turn so that the kick goes to the defensive zone.

• When contesting a loose ball in the back lines, back players should try and force the ball towards the boundary and not back into play.

• At boundary throw-ins, the ruckman should attempt to bring the ball to ground forward of the pack close to the boundary line. He should never try to hit the ball back over his head into the opponent's scoring zone.

• Kicking across goals is risky. However, it can be an effective way to establish an attack by switching the attack's direction. This is gener-

ally done deep in defense, where the ball is driven wide to the opposite defensive zone. Doing this, players need to kick the ball long, so that the receiver does not have to come back to meet the ball and so an inaccurate kick runs towards the boundary line, away from the opponent's attacking zone.

• Defensive players position themselves between their opponents and the goal to force attackers to turn towards the defensive flank and away from the team's scoring zone. This position also forces the attacking player to lead to the outside.

• When pursuing an attacking player, the defender should try and chase from the inside and force the attacker towards the boundary (see Figure 12.4). This prevents easy access to the scoring zone.

• A defensive player should determine which side his opponent prefers for disposal and anticipate moves to that side. Forcing an opponent onto his 'wrong' leg and away from the scoring zone is effective defense.

• Ruckmen will try and move back into the free space in front of the opposing key forwards in the scoring zone. This reduces the options available for the forwards to lead and forces them to move into the defensive flanks. This positioning also causes those delivering the ball to kick it high, thus making it easier to spoil.

• When a forward has possession in the defensive zones defenders should anticipate a kick to the scoring zone. This is particularly important in situations where the attackers have a free kick or a mark in this area. They may kick the ball backwards to gain a better position. Good defense will force the player to kick for goal from his poor position.

IN ATTACK

• In attack, players usually position themselves so that their preferred foot will naturally kick the ball into the attacking zone when making a turn.

• Attackers usually start from the defensive zones of the opposition and their leads take them into the scoring zone.

• To create space in the attacking area the half forwards often play up the field and lead back towards goal.

• On taking possession, players should attempt to turn so that their kick will go into the scoring zone.

• The ball should be centered whenever possible. From the flanks the ball should be kicked to the head of the kickoff square.

• Space can be created in the attacking zone by leading out to the flank and then doubling back. This can be done by one player making a dummy lead out of the scoring zone and another player leading into the space created.

• It is important not to crowd the scoring zone. Centre line players should not go into this

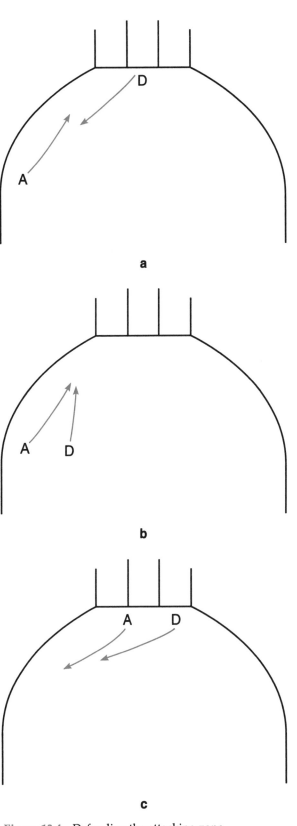

Figure 12.4   Defending the attacking zone.

area too soon. It is better to go in at the same time as the ball and read it off hands or take the handball at your top speed.

• The ball should be moved forward into the attacking area quickly before defensive ruckmen and centre players can crowd the scoring space.

• Coming out of defense, do not centre the ball too early. An interception will give the opponent good attacking position.

• The ruckman will try and knock some of the boundary throw-ins back into the scoring zone. At other times he will try and get the ball to players moving into the scoring zone.

• Forward players should anticipate their defensive opponents trying to clear the ball to the flanks. They should try to block this movement and force them to kick the ball to the middle of the field.

RUCKWORK

The game is started at each quarter and restarted after each goal by a bounce in the centre circle. Only four players from each team may be in the square until the ball touches the ground. This controlled situation allows for set plays to be used in taking the ball out of the square. There are many such plays but they are based on three strategies.

• *Man on man*. Here a team decides that it will simply man up on opponents in the square (Figure 12.5). A team usually uses this tactic if it has good ball getters in the square or as a defensive move if the other team is getting the ball out of the square too often.

• *Zoned placement*. Each of the four players controls a specific area (Figure 12.6). Usually the follower positions on the defensive side of the circle towards the back of the square to cover the ball coming out. The rover is placed 'on the ruckman's arm'—that is, where the ruckman expects to put the ball. The centre player is usually on the attacking side of the circle to assist the rover or to defend if the opponents take possession in this area.

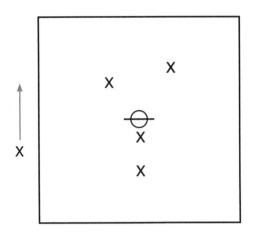

Figure 12.6   Zoned placement positioning.

• *Check side placement*. Here a team concedes that the opposition ruckman is likely to win the knock and place it in a particular area. The team places players in that area and their own ruckman also tries to get the ball to that position (Figure 12.7).

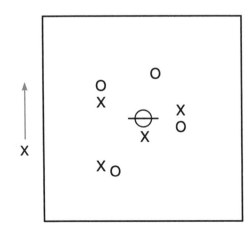

Figure 12.5   Man on man positioning.

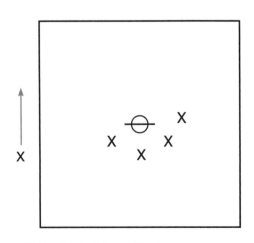

Figure 12.7   Check side positioning.

A common combination of these tactics is to place the rover on the ruckman's arm, the follower covering the zone on the defensive side of the circle and the centreman going man on man on the opposition rover (Figure 12.8).

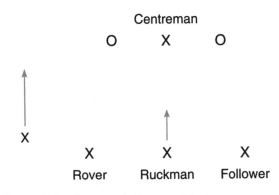

Figure 12.8   Common ball up positioning.

When there is a ball up following a scrimmage the tactics are not as clear cut because more players are about the ball and the bounce can be at any position on the field. Generally in this situation a check side is used. The tactic is that the follower and rover position themselves between the bounce and their opponent's goal. The ruckman attempts to bring the ball back giving them possession as they move straight towards their own goal. If the opposition gets the knock the rover and follower are already moving towards them for a tackle or smother, which will force the opponents to run wide to

attack. A position player will need to be stationed within the opposition to try and prevent them from taking possession.

An adaption of this tactic is used for boundary throw-ins, where the ruckman attempts to put the ball down to the check (defensive) side so that when the ball is taken the players' movement is in the direction of the goals. The ensuing movement depends on whether the throw-in is in attack or defense. In defense the players try to keep the ball close to the boundary by the ruckman knocking forward (see Figure 12.9a). In attack he will attempt to hit to the side or the back so that once the ball is gathered it can be taken inside to a better scoring position (see Figure 12.9b). In all cases it is vital to have at least one position player stationed among the opposition to defend and another to cover the back of the pack to defend the hit there.

THE KICKOFF

The only other time during the game that set plays can be planned is when the ball is kicked out after a behind has been scored. Here there are several options.

Any player can kick off. (It has already been established that the ball is usually kicked wide to the defensive flanks out of the opponent's scoring zone.) The long kick is directed to the leading player moving from the midline of the field to the flank. If the team has a strong mark it is usual to play towards him. The opposition will try to counter this, so another option needs

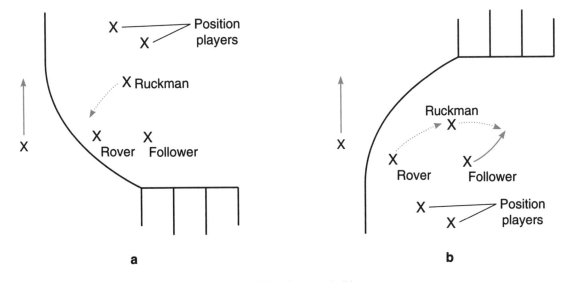

Figure 12.9   Boundary throw-ins tactic: in defense (a) and in attack (b).

to be available. If the opposition has a dominant marking player it is of course good sense to kick it away from him.

The short kick to a player (usually a winger, back pocket or half back who leads to the pocket) is a good way of establishing an attacking play by creating a loose man, particularly if the alert player runs past the receiver, takes the ball back and then kicks it long.

Figure 12.10 illustrates the concept of 'making space' for a kickoff, which is an important team tactic. Teams may group together and prior to kickoff scatter into spaces where the ball will be kicked. A variation of this is to designate a player to make a dummy lead to create space into which the ball will be kicked as another player moves into that space.

The player kicking off can kick the ball to himself provided it goes over the kickoff line and travels a minimum of 2 metres. Because the full forward must be back from the head of the kickoff square, the player kicking off has an advantage (particularly if this tactic is employed close to the goal line) and can run the ball out of the area to create the loose man or to kick the ball over the waiting pack to a player running into attack.

If in doubt as to where to kick the ball, or if there is a following wind, the player kicking off will probably kick the ball as far as possible to the defensive zones or straight down the middle to get as close as possible to his team's attacking zone.

Defense of the kickoff is either player on player or, if the opposition is grouping, cover zones (see Figure 12.11).

USE OF CONDITIONS

A good team adapts its game plan and tactics to the weather. Adverse conditions will affect both teams, and the team best able to adapt will have an advantage. The element that affects the game most is the wind, as the flight of the ball is noticeably affected.

A following wind carries a kick a greater distance, making it imperative that there are players on the ground behind the pack to take the falling ball off hands. Kicking with the wind is an advantage that needs to be capitalised on. Generally the ball is kicked long, straight and quickly. A mistake can be in taking the wind for granted. Even with wind, kicks need to be directed to players and spaces; the main difference is that with a following wind the kicker can look further afield for his target.

When defending against the wind, it is best to slow the game down and keep the ball wide on the ground. Attacking against the wind, though difficult, often results in good team football because the game becomes one of running, sharing and possession. The ball is carried into the wind by low trajectory kicks and handpasses combined with running the ball using several teammates.

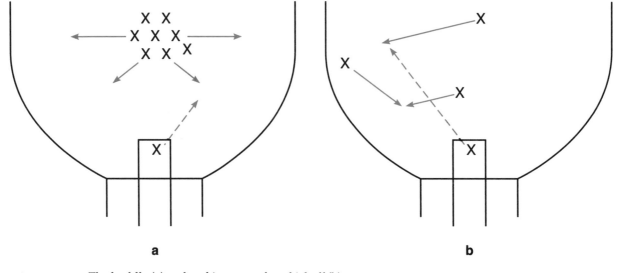

Figure 12.10   The huddle (a) and making space for a kickoff (b).

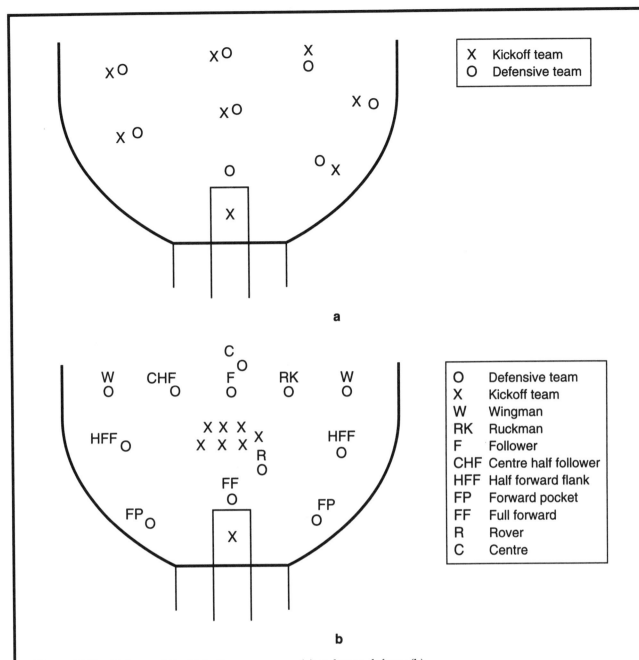

Figure 12.11   Defense of the kickoff: man-on-man (a) and zone defense (b).

READING THE PLAY

Because basic tactics form most game plans, they are used by both teams. Hence a team often suspects what an opponent will do in a given situation. Of course the opposition is aware of these suspicions and will sometimes alter its tactics in an attempt to catch the other team by surprise. Here is where the glorious uncertainty of sport takes over and where superior skill (and some luck) influences the result. An important skill in most sports, including Australian football, is the ability to read a play. This skill involves understanding the basic tactics of the game, incorporating knowledge of teammates' and opponents' strengths and weaknesses and responding to information coming in on things like the flight of the ball, the weather, the condition of the ground, positions of other players,

A cross wind often results in low-scoring, tight games. In these conditions consider the zones to have been moved across the field towards the wind, as shown in Figure 12.12. That is, players defend to the leeward side of the ground and attack from the windward side.

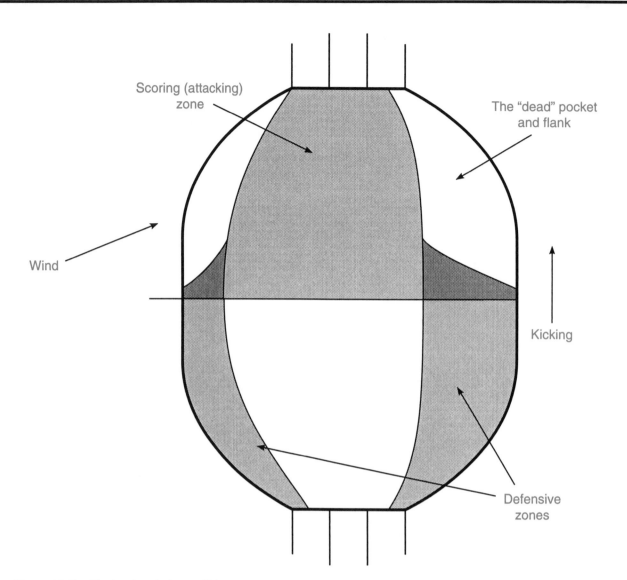

Figure 12.12   Playing in windy conditions.

THE TEAM PLAYER

the type of kick used and the like. Processing all this information enables the player to anticipate where the ball is going, perhaps even while it is still a kick or two away. This skill varies from player to player but can be improved by all through practice, attention to detail and, above all, concentration.

Team play is more than tactics and strategies. Good teams are made up of individuals endeavouring to play their part in advantaging their teammates and disadvantaging the opposition. All players can contribute to their team's success in the way they approach the game and by following guidelines established by the team and the coach. The good team player possesses a variety of qualities.

• He is committed, confident and disciplined.

• He goes to meet the ball and does not wait for it to come to him. His approach on the ball is straight and aggressive. His approach on the player is equally as straight and hard but is also legal (a player who gives away needless free kicks is not a good team player).

• He talks to his teammates. Not every player will be outgoing, but a team player needs to let his teammates know what is going on around them as they go for the ball. Talk should always be positive and encouraging.

- He knows his own strengths and weaknesses as well as those of teammates and the opposition.

- He recovers his position after a play so that an intercepted ball is not easily sent back to his uncontested opponent.

- He moves back quickly to take his kick from a mark or free kick and does not turn his back on the play. This enables him to look for options to kick, handball or play on.

- He will man up on his opponent whenever his opponent has the ball.

- He recovers quickly after falling. A player on the ground is a noncontributing player.

- He won't allow a teammate going for the ball to be outnumbered. He positions to back him up, talks to him and protects him by shepherding.

- He kicks long to position or to the moving player and kicks short only when possession to a teammate is virtually assured.

- He doesn't consider his job done once he has disposed of the ball. He runs past to be in a position to receive the ball back if necessary, backs up his teammate in case of a fumble, blocks and shepherds his teammate to allow him to dispose without pressure and then gets back to his position to cover his opponent.

- He takes front position over the ball. This is where he will get the free kicks.

- He will get down to the ball in packs and knock it out to teammates, through for a point or to the boundary.

- He chases an opponent when there is little or no chance of catching him but when the chase may cause a fumble or a ball-handling error.

- He spoils and doesn't attempt to mark when out of position.

- He doesn't allow a ruckman, follower or rover to stand a mark or free kick.

Team Drills

Many drills have been developed to practise team plays. These drills are the essence of the team discipline that coaches demand of their players. Generally the drills cannot be done alone or even in small groups; they are usually kept until formal practice. However, what follows are a few drills you can try if you have five or six friends who want to improve basic team patterns to make themselves better team players. In several

of these, Success Goals are not identified, nor is there a requirement to keep your score. Generally, the object of the drills is to allow you many attempts at practising concepts of team play, team disciplines and movement patterns. For each of the drills, make the distances between players and size of the field appropriate to the size and skill of the players practising.

1. Head of the Square

Remember that the object of good forward team play is to get the ball into the best possible scoring position—usually directly in front of the goals. Player A rolls the ball in the direction of and close to the boundary. Player B runs after the ball, picks it up and—instead of trying to kick the goal from an almost impossible angle—kicks it high to the 'head of the square' for Player C to mark. Change positions after each kick; have 10 kicks each.

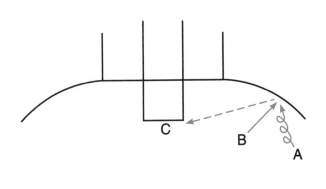

Success Goal = Your kicks are marked in the goal square 10 times out of 10

Your Score = (#) _____ kicks marked in the square

Try this drill again from the other side of the goals.

Success Goal = Your kicks are marked in the goal square 8 times out of 10 (because you will probably now be practising with your 'wrong' foot)

Your Score = (#) _____ kicks marked in the square

2. The Handball Option

If a player is facing the opposite direction to which his team is attacking, upon receiving the ball he shouldn't have to turn and kick. It is good team play for teammates to run past him for the handball. Try this drill in a group of five. Player A kicks the ball to Player B who marks it as Player C runs past. Player C calls for the handball and then kicks to Player D. Player D now kicks the ball to A who has taken C's position and B runs past A, gets the handball, kicks to Player E and the process starts again.

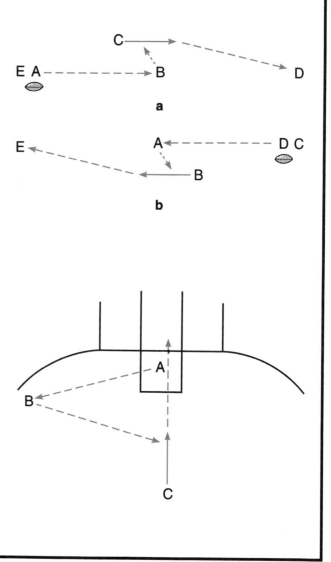

3. Defend and Score

In kicking away from goal a defender usually tries to go close to the boundary line. Attackers try to get the ball towards the midline of the ground to score. In this drill Player A, defending, kicks the ball to B who is close to the boundary line. Player B passes to C who has run from near the centre to take the ball and run straight at goal to try a shot. Follow the ball to the next position. Here it is important for A to get the ball close to the boundary and B to get his pass in front of C so C can kick the goal.

4. Cover the Turn Over

A player takes a risk and leaves his opponent to attack. However, if the ball is intercepted, the good team player will make every endeavour to get back to cover his opponent. Player A kicks the ball to B (who marks it) and races after it to receive a handball back from B. He then kicks the ball to D who plays the part of the intercepting player. Player A then has to turn and sprint back to his starting point before D kicks the ball to B, runs past for the handball from B and kicks to E. In other words, A has to beat the ball back to E. Player E now becomes the intercepting player and has to get the ball to B and beat D back to his starting point. Have 5 tries each at beating the ball back. Score a point each time you beat the ball back to your starting position but subtract 2 points if your kick couldn't be marked (intercepted).

Success Goal = 5 points from 5 tries

Your Score = (#) ____ points

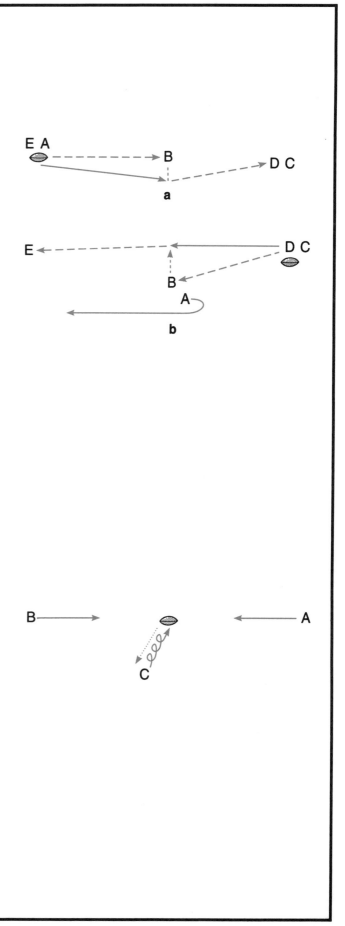

5. Tap It On

It is often impossible to take the ball and handball to a teammate. In such cases it is good play to knock the ball out in front of him so that he can pick it up under less pressure. Player C rolls the ball between A and B but closer to A than B. Player A gets to the ball first and knocks it back to C who is able to pick it up. Score 1 point each time the ball is knocked back to C. Have five tries in each position.

Success Goal = Player A should be able to get 5 out of 5 (because A has an advantage and B is merely trying to stop the knock on)

Your Score = (#) ____ points when you are Player A

6. *Give and Go*

Too often players handball or kick the ball and think that their job is done. This drill requires the player who has given the handball to chase after it and try to execute a tackle. The players are in groups of five. Player A handballs to B who handballs to C who handballs to D who handballs to E. All players are running forward to the markers except for A who runs behind the group trying to get close enough to E to tackle him before he reaches the marker. Change positions after each run with each player having several turns at being the chaser and the chased.

Success Goal = To catch Player E when you are A

Your Score =

(#) _____ times you caught Player E

(#) _____ times you did not catch Player E

7. *Run Inside*

On the diagram of the football field the attacking zone is in the middle. In actual play there is often space to the outside, and players run here to the disadvantage of their team. Players should get into the habit early of running inside. In this drill A kicks to B who marks and handballs to C who has run inside to take the ball and kick the goal. To get the ball back to the starting position D kicks to E on the boundary line and E runs up to take the place of A. In the meanwhile Player A becomes B, B becomes C, C becomes D and D becomes E.

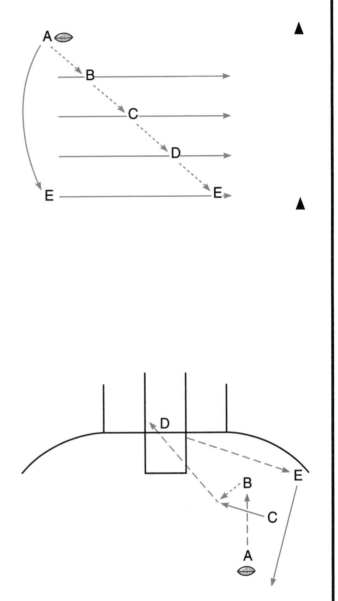

8. *Kick, Mark, Handball*

In Handball Option (#2) players run past the marking player facing the wrong direction. A potent piece of attacking team play is to handball forward to a running player, often enabling the next kick to clear defenders who have set themselves to intercept. In this drill, A kicks high to B who marks and handballs to either C or D as they run forward. The receiving player then kicks to the middle person of the next group, and the process is repeated. After each mark and handball all three players involved run to the other end of the drill.

9. *Kickoff Drill*

Have one player play the part of the full back kicking off. Other players huddle together until the full back is ready to kick off. As the full back prepares to kick off, all other players sprint in various directions to give many targets for the kickoff. The full back tries to get the ball on the full or in front of one of the running players.

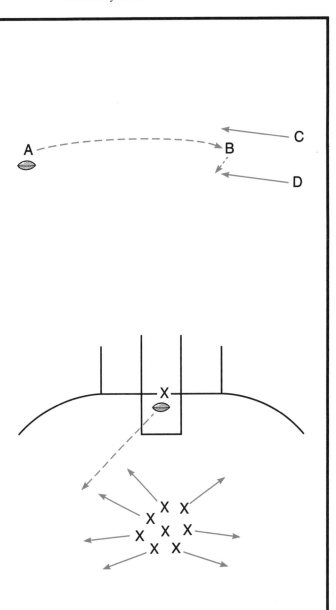

10. Six Stations

Six players practise defensive and offensive use of the football field. Player A kicks the ball to B who is leading towards the defensive edge of the field. Player C runs past for a handball and kicks the ball down the side of the field to D who is leading into the attacking corridor. Player D handballs to E who is running straight at goal and has a shot. Player F recovers the ball and starts the ball back in the other direction with all players taking reverse roles. After the ball goes back to the start, A, B and C change positions as do D, E and F. Don't use all of the football ground. It is too long. Put in your own markers to act as goals so that they can be reached without too much running and bouncing between stations.

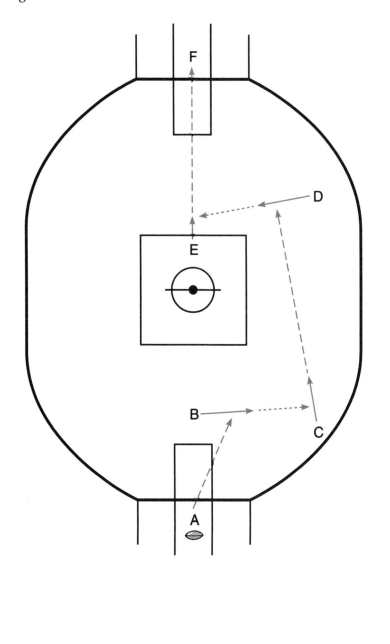

11. Goal Race

Divide your group into two teams, each with its own ball. On a signal, the two teams kick the ball off from the kickoff square and try to be the first to score a goal at the other end of the ground. Score 1 point for being first to score. In taking the ball down the ground each team must stay on its side of the ground and not go into the centre square. After each goal and when both teams are ready, another signal is given and the race is repeated in the opposite direction. First team to score 5 points wins.

Success Goal = Scoring 5 points before the opposing team

Your Score =

    (#) _____ points scored by your team

    (#) _____ points scored by opposing team

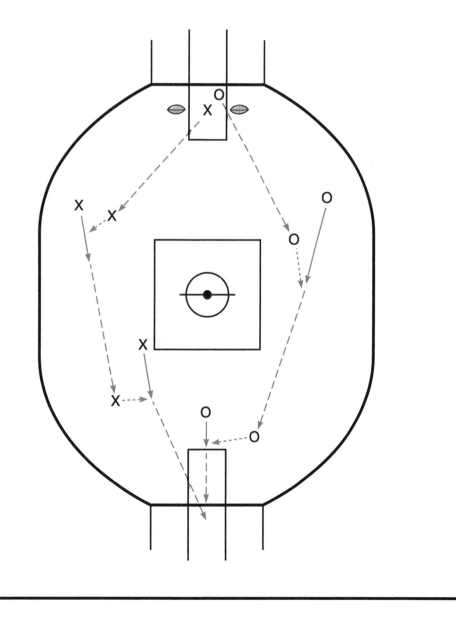

Step 13   Know the Rules

The rules of any game are meant to create order. Umpires interpret and apply rules during a game. Australian football is controlled by six umpires—two central or field umpires, two boundary umpires and two goal umpires. Umpires, players, coaches and indeed spectators need to know the rules and understand their spirit as well as some of the difficulties in their application. Many of the rules in Australian football are open to interpretation; rules pertaining to scoring and whether the ball is in or out of play depend on the judgement of the umpires.

As Bill Deller, the National Director of Umpiring has said:

> Umpiring Australian football is the most difficult adjudicating task in the world. The game is played on the biggest of all sporting arenas; it has the largest number of players; it is the fastest moving and allows more physical contact . . . over a longer time period than any other football code. Added to this, the laws are interpretive and the umpire is continually called upon to make judgements. . . . The fact that the laws are so interpretive is a unique feature of the game.*

All serious players should have a copy of the official rules of the game. These are available from the various state football leagues and associations or directly from the National Football Council of Australia. The following is a summary of the main playing rules.

THE GAME

At senior level the game is played over 4 quarters of 20 minutes each, with time being added on for delay of game, player injury, recovery of the ball due to scoring and 'out of bounds'. This 'time on' will be signalled by the central umpires but recorded and added to normal time by the time-keepers.

The game is started at each quarter and restarted after each goal by one of the central um-

pires bouncing or throwing the ball up in the centre circle. At this time only four players from each team are permitted in the centre square and no player may be in the centre circle until the ball is bounced. Infringements to these rules result in a free kick to the opposition from the centre circle.

After a behind has been scored, any player from the defending team kicks the ball back into play from within the kickoff lines in front of goal. At this time the ball must travel a minimum of 2 metres before the kicker can take the ball again (this is rarely seen, however; most kickoffs are kicked long out of the scoring area) with all other players being at least 5 metres from the kickoff line when the ball is kicked.

If the ball goes out of bounds other than on the full from a kick or directly from a kickoff without being touched by any player, a boundary umpire throws the ball back over his head towards the centre of the ground into play. If the ball goes out of bounds on the full from a kick, either directly from kickoff or from being deliberately knocked or carried over the boundary line, a free kick is awarded to the nearest player from the opposite team.

SCORING

A goal (6 points) is scored when the ball is kicked over the goal line by a player of the attacking team without the ball touching a player or goal post.

A behind (1 point) is scored when the ball passes over the goal line in any way other than just described, touches or passes over a goal post or passes over a behind line without touching or passing over a behind post. A defending player cannot score a goal for the opposition—if he kicks or takes the ball over either the goal or behind lines, a behind is scored for the attacking team.

To score, the ball must completely cross the goal line. To go out of bounds, the ball must completely cross the boundary line.

---

*Note. From *NAFC Level 2 Coaching Manual* by J. Warren (Ed.), 1991, Melbourne: National Australian Football Council.

GAINING POSSESSION

The 'Spirit of The Laws' statement relating to possession says in the official rules:

> The player who makes the ball his sole objective shall be given every opportunity to gain possession of the ball. (12.1)

This statement is intended to help players and umpires in the interpretation and application of the rules of football.

A mark is allowed when the ball is caught on the full from a kick that has travelled at least 10 metres and is not touched in flight. The player taking the mark may go back 'behind the mark' and take his kick or may play on immediately. In going for a mark a player may be awarded a free kick if he is

- blocked or shepherded when the ball is more than 5 metres away;
- pushed, bumped or shepherded when he is in the air attempting a mark;
- pushed from behind except when the opponent is legitimately attempting to mark, spoil or play the ball;
- held, tripped or charged by an opponent or
- hit on the head, neck or top of the shoulders by an opponent trying to contest the mark.

In general play, in contesting for possession of the ball a player will be awarded a free kick when he is

- held in any way when not in possession of the ball;
- shepherded when the ball is not within 5 metres;
- pushed from behind in any way;
- tripped, charged, struck or kicked;
- pushed, bumped or shepherded in the face, head, neck or on the shoulders;
- in possession of the ball and tackled below the knees or on or above the shoulders including the collar of the football uniform or
- held once he has legally disposed of the ball.

IN POSSESSION

Once a player possesses the ball rules pertain to that possession. Again, the statement relating to the Spirit of The Law helps in the understanding, interpretation and application of these rules.

> The player who has possession of the ball and is held by an opponent shall be given a reasonable time to kick or handball the ball. (12.2)

A player is deemed to be in possession of the ball if he is holding the ball, bouncing it while running or lying on or over the ball. He may possess the ball for an unlimited time provided he is not held by an opponent. If he is running with the ball, he must bounce it or touch it on the ground once every 15 metres. Once tackled, however, the player in possession must attempt to dispose of the ball *immediately* by kicking or handballing. A player in possession of the ball will have a free kick awarded against him for

- not disposing of the ball within a reasonable time when held by an opponent;
- dropping the ball or bouncing it when tackled;
- holding the ball if he has the ball pinned or held to him by a tackle and has had a reasonable chance to dispose of the ball prior to being tackled;
- throwing or handing off the ball (the ball must be held in one hand and hit with the clenched fist of the other hand);
- kicking the ball over the boundary line on the full without it being touched by another player (here the free kick is awarded where the ball crosses over the boundary line rather than where the kick was taken);
- deliberately forcing the ball over the boundary line or
- running more than 15 metres with the ball without touching or bouncing it on the ground.

In most cases, the free kicks are taken at the spot where the infringement took place. An exception is where a player is infringed against after he has disposed of the ball; here a 'foul after disposal' will result in a free kick from where the ball landed. (If the kick has scored a behind the infringed player is given the choice of accepting the score or having another kick.) Under the Spirit of The Laws, the central umpires can allow play to continue after an infraction (even though a free kick should have been awarded) when stopping play would penalise the team offended. This is indicated by the umpire calling 'play on!' and applies only to free kicks, not to marks.

In the same spirit, to keep the ball and game moving and to prevent time wasting and the deliberate professional foul', a central umpire may award a 50-metre penalty following a mark or free kick if in his opinion

- a player is infringed against after a mark or free kick has been awarded;
- the player on the mark refuses to stand on the mark or encroaches over the mark;
- the player deliberately wastes time by knocking the ball away from the player who has been awarded a free kick or who has marked the ball or by not returning the ball on the full to the player who is to take the kick or
- the player on the mark holds the player who is to take the kick.

On many fields a semi-circle of 50-metre radius is drawn from the centre of the goal line. This serves no purpose other than to give the umpires a reference when applying a 50-metre penalty.

RULES RELATING TO TAKING THE FREE KICK OR A KICK FROM A MARK

When a player takes his kick, only one opponent is allowed to 'stand the mark'. No other player is allowed within a 10-metre-radius semicircle behind the mark (see Figure 13.1).

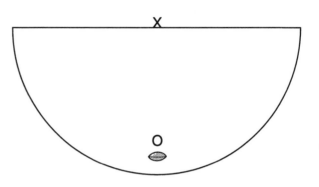

Figure 13.1   Player X stands the mark; Player O has the free kick or mark.

When kicking, the umpire will direct the player to kick 'over his mark'. However, if and when the player moves off the direct line over the mark to the goal, the umpire will call 'play on' and defensive players may attempt a tackle.

HOW WELL DO YOU KNOW THE RULES?

What is the umpire's decision? Score 1 point for each correct answer.

1. Player A tackles Player B, firmly pinning his arms to his sides. Player B drops the ball.

2. Player A has taken a mark and Player B comes in and knocks the ball out of his hands.

3. Player A hands (gives) the ball to his teammate while being tackled by Player B.

4. Player A holds the ball for longer than 5 seconds but is not tackled.

5. Player A runs 10 metres, handballs over Player B's head, retakes the ball without it hitting the ground and runs another 10 metres before kicking.

6. The full back kicks out after a behind and the ball goes over the boundary line without anyone touching it.

7. Player A leaps from behind Player B and pushes with his hands on Player B's shoulders to get more height and take a spectacular mark.

8. Player A has the ball and is about to be tackled by Player B. Just before the tackle, Player A bounces the ball and does not have it in his hands when tackled by Player B.

9. Player A is running towards the boundary line chased by Player B. He slips and while falling knocks the ball over the boundary line so that Player B cannot get it.

10. Player A is tackled around the neck and the ball drops to the ground. His teammate, Player B, picks up the ball and kicks it down the ground in the direction of another teammate.

11. The ball is halfway across the boundary line but is knocked back by a player before it completely crosses the line.

12. Player A, while desperately defending, turns and kicks with the ball coming off the side of his foot and going through his opponent's goals.

13. Player A marks the ball and goes back to take his kick. As he runs in to take his kick he slips, falls and drops the ball, which an opponent picks up.

14. Player A marks the ball and goes back to take his kick. He sees a teammate and makes to give a handball but changes his mind and does not release the ball.

15. The ball is kicked at goal and goes directly over the goal post. What does the goal umpire signal?

Success Goal = 15 correct responses out of 15

Your Score = (#) _____ correct responses

ANSWERS TO QUIZ ON RULES

1. Holding the ball. Free kick to A.
2. Award A the mark and charge B a 50-metre penalty.
3. Free kick to B. The ball cannot be handed to a teammate. It must be hand passed by punching the ball.
4. Play on.
5. Running too far without the ball touching the ground. Free kick to B.
6. Free kick to opposition from where the ball crossed the boundary.
7. No mark. Free kick to B for interference above shoulder.
8. Holding the ball against A, who is deemed to be in possession. Free kick to B.
9. If it is accidental, throw in. If the umpire interprets that it was deliberately hit over the boundary line, free kick to B.
10. Free kick to A for over the shoulder but play on for team's advantage.
11. Play on because the ball did not completely cross the boundary line.
12. One point scored for the opponents.
13. If the umpire has not called 'play on' and Player A is still behind his mark, he retakes his kick.
14. The umpire will call 'play on' and Player A can be tackled.
15. One point (a behind) as the ball must clearly go between the goal posts or their extension.

Rating Your Total Progress

To play Australian football successfully you need to learn the basic skills and understand team plans and strategies. You should also know the rules of the game. You have now had a chance to learn the skills and to apply them to practice in skill-testing drills. You have learned some of the fundamental strategies and the basic rules of the game. Now, how would you rate yourself on the following? With the skills, grade yourself as *very good* only if you are able to do the skill with both your left and right hand (or foot). Remember: A good player is a two-sided player. If you are confident of your ability to perform the skill effectively, grade yourself as *good. Okay* suggests the need for improvement, particularly when using the nonpreferred hand or foot or when under pressure. *Poor* means that you are still having difficulty and need to work on the skill to correct errors.

PHYSICAL SKILLS

	Very Good	Good	Okay	Poor
Handball Skills				
Basic handball	_____	_____	_____	_____
Tumble handball	_____	_____	_____	_____
Rocket handball	_____	_____	_____	_____
Gathering Skills				
Stationary ball	_____	_____	_____	_____
Oncoming ball				
Rolling	_____	_____	_____	_____
Bouncing	_____	_____	_____	_____
Ball leaving you				
Rolling	_____	_____	_____	_____
Bouncing	_____	_____	_____	_____
Marking Skills				
Chest mark	_____	_____	_____	_____
Low chest mark	_____	_____	_____	_____
Overhead mark	_____	_____	_____	_____
Forward hand mark	_____	_____	_____	_____
Kicking Skills				
Flat punt	_____	_____	_____	_____
Drop punt	_____	_____	_____	_____
Torpedo punt	_____	_____	_____	_____
Reverse punt	_____	_____	_____	_____
Running and Bouncing				
Bouncing the ball	_____	_____	_____	_____
Running and bouncing	_____	_____	_____	_____
Baulk	_____	_____	_____	_____
Blind turn	_____	_____	_____	_____
Double-back	_____	_____	_____	_____
Ruckwork				
Centre bounce	_____	_____	_____	_____
Throw-in	_____	_____	_____	_____
Defensive Skills				
Tackling	_____	_____	_____	_____
Bumping	_____	_____	_____	_____
Shepherding	_____	_____	_____	_____
Smothering the ball	_____	_____	_____	_____
Spoiling the ball	_____	_____	_____	_____
Standing the mark	_____	_____	_____	_____

FITNESS LEVEL

A good player is a fit player. How would you rate your fitness for Australian football under the following headings?

	Very Good	Good	Okay	Poor
Speed	_____	_____	_____	_____
Flexibility	_____	_____	_____	_____
Power	_____	_____	_____	_____
Strength	_____	_____	_____	_____
Agility	_____	_____	_____	_____
Stamina	_____	_____	_____	_____

KNOWLEDGE OF THE RULES

How well do you know the rules? If you were called upon to umpire a game how well would you be able to interpret and apply the following rules?

	Very Well	Well	Okay	Not So Well
A mark	_____	_____	_____	_____
Throw	_____	_____	_____	_____
Holding the ball	_____	_____	_____	_____
Holding the man	_____	_____	_____	_____
Over the shoulder	_____	_____	_____	_____
Push in the back	_____	_____	_____	_____
Out on the full	_____	_____	_____	_____
Kickoff	_____	_____	_____	_____
Centre square control	_____	_____	_____	_____
Standing the mark	_____	_____	_____	_____
Interference	_____	_____	_____	_____
Possession	_____	_____	_____	_____
Play on	_____	_____	_____	_____
A goal	_____	_____	_____	_____
A behind	_____	_____	_____	_____
Out of bounds	_____	_____	_____	_____
50-metre penalty	_____	_____	_____	_____

KNOWLEDGE OF BASIC TEAM STRATEGIES

How well do you know the basic team strategies?

On a sheet of paper place and name the 21 players of a football team.

Draw an oval and mark in the attacking and defensive zones what a team has to keep in mind.

List 10 qualities that go towards making a player a good team man.

Draw a diagram to show where the ruckman will place his teammates and try to direct the ball for ruck contests from a bounce and from throw-ins.

OVERALL FOOTBALL PROGRESS

Considering all the checklisted items how would you rate your overall progress?

Very successful	_____
Successful	_____
Fairly successful	_____
Just satisfactory	_____
Unsatisfactory	_____

ADDITIONAL COMMENTS AND QUESTIONS

Review your self-ratings. What are your strong points? What are your weaker points? How can you improve your performance? Are you willing to spend the time and effort needed to improve your game?

Individual Program

INDIVIDUAL COURSE IN _____

STUDENT'S NAME _____

GRADE/COURSE SECTION _____

STUDENT ID # _____

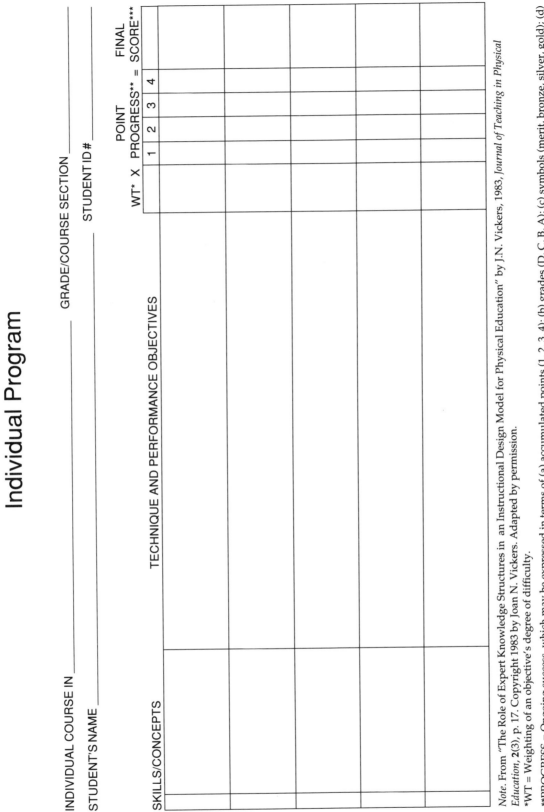

SKILLS/CONCEPTS	TECHNIQUE AND PERFORMANCE OBJECTIVES	WT* X	POINT PROGRESS**				FINAL = SCORE***
			1	2	3	4	

Note. From "The Role of Expert Knowledge Structures in an Instructional Design Model for Physical Education" by J.N. Vickers, 1983, *Journal of Teaching in Physical Education*, **2**(3), p. 17. Copyright 1983 by Joan N. Vickers. Adapted by permission.

*WT = Weighting of an objective's degree of difficulty.

**PROGRESS = Ongoing success, which may be expressed in terms of (a) accumulated points (1, 2, 3, 4); (b) grades (D, C, B, A); (c) symbols (merit, bronze, silver, gold); (d) unsatisfactory/satisfactory; and others as desired.

***FINAL SCORE equals WT times PROGRESS.

Glossary

As I've pointed out in the text of this book, Australian football is a unique game. In common with most games it has its own language that players and spectators understand but it is quite strange to those unfamiliar with it. What follows is a list of some of the more common words and expressions used in Australian football. Understanding these terms is crucial for players and helpful for spectators.

backmen—The six defenders across the full back and half back lines who are placed in a team's defensive half of the field.

back pocket—The position on either side of the full back on the last line of defense.

ball up—When the central umpire bounces or throws up the ball to restart the game after a scrimmage that results in a stalemate with neither team having an advantage.

baulk—A player with the ball attempting to deceive his opponent by faking a move in one direction and suddenly going in another.

behind—When the ball passes over the goal line after being touched or kicked by a defender, when it hits a goal post or when it passes over the behind line without touching the behind post. A behind scores 1 point.

behind line—The line drawn between a goal post and behind post.

behind posts—The two smaller posts 6.4 metres outside the goal posts.

boundary line—The line that marks the boundary of the playing field. The ball must go completely over the line to be out of bounds.

boundary umpires—Two of these umpires patrol the boundary line, one on each side of the field. They judge whether the ball is in play or not. When the ball is out of play, they return it to play by throwing it in over their heads towards the centre of the field.

bump—When a player uses his hip and shoulder to knock an opponent out of position. To be legitimate a bump must not be in the back or above the shoulders of the opponent and must be made within 5 metres of the ball.

central umpire—Also called the field umpire. There are two on the ground during a game. They have full control of play and award penalties in accordance with the rules of the game.

centre bounce—The umpire's bounce of the ball in the centre circle to start the game at the beginning of each quarter and to restart it after each goal.

centre circle—The 3-metre-diameter circle in the centre of the ground where the ball is bounced by the central umpire to start and restart the game. No player is to be in the centre circle until the ball has been bounced (or left the umpire's hand if he is throwing it up).

centre square—The 45-metre square in the centre of the ground to control the number of players around the ball at a centre bounce. Only four players from each team are permitted in the centre square at a centre bounce.

centre the ball—Directing the ball into an attacking position on the field directly in front of the goals.

check side—The defensive side of a contest. Usually referred to in relation to a ruck contest.

crumber—See **off hands/off the pack**.

dead pocket—A defensive area of the ground near a behind post where the ball is likely to be blown on a windy day.

downfield—Towards a team's goal.

dropping the ball—When a player is tackled and drops the ball, giving a free kick to the tackler. The spectators will call 'ball!' in anticipation of the umpire awarding the free kick.

drop punt—The kick most often used in Australian football. In flight it will spin end over end backwards.

fall of the ball—Where the ball is expected to come to ground following a kick. Rovers, followers and other running players will attempt to be at the fall of the ball to gather it as it comes off hands and dispose of it to their team's advantage.

fifty-metre circle—On many grounds a semi-circle of 50-metre radius is drawn from the centre of each goal. There are no rules directly relating to these and they are drawn solely to help umpires judge 50 metres for awarding a 50-metre penalty.

first give—When a player takes the first option to dispose of the ball to a teammate. In senior football not to do this will often lead to the player with the ball being caught holding the ball and giving away a free kick.

flank—The part of the ground near the boundary line between the pocket and the wings.

followers—The team's ruckman, ruck rover and rover.

footpass—When the ball is passed to a teammate by kicking.

forwards—The six players of the full forward and half forward lines who are placed in a team's attacking half of the field.

free kick—The awarding of a penalty kick for an infringement of the rules. In fact, the ball does not have to be kicked but may be handpassed. If by making the infringed team take its kick it would be disadvantaged, the umpire may call 'play on!' and allow the play to continue.

game plan—The strategies developed by the coach to maximise team strengths and to counter the opposition's. Will involve team disciplines developed during training.

gathering the ball—Taking possession of the ball that has fallen free from a marking or ruck contest or is rolling free on the ground.

goal—A goal is worth 6 points and is scored when the ball is kicked over the goal line by a player of the attacking team without the ball touching any player or a goal post.

goal line—The line drawn between the goal posts.

goal mouth—The area directly between the goal posts in front of goal.

goal posts—The two posts 6.4 metres apart between which the ball is kicked to score a goal worth 6 points.

goal square—The 6.4 metre × 9 metre rectangle in front of the goal posts from which the ball is kicked off after a behind is scored. The lines of the 'square' make up the kickoff lines.

goal umpires—Umpires who judge the scoring of goals and behinds and record the scores. They signal a goal by waving two flags and a behind by waving one.

half-volley take—Where the ball is gathered by the player as it hits the ground.

handball—Holding the ball in one hand and hitting it with the clenched fist of the other hand. (Also called a handpass.)

head of the square—Where players on an acute angle to the goal will try and kick the ball rather than have a shot at goal. The head of the square is the part of the goal square closest to the centre of the ground.

hit out—Where players contesting a bounce, ball up or throw-in try to hit the ball to a teammate.

hit the post—Where the ball in flight hits one of the posts. If it hits a goal post, a behind is scored. If it hits a behind post, it is ruled out of bounds.

holding the ball—When tackled the player in possession of the ball does not dispose of it legally in a reasonable time and has a free kick awarded against him. Spectators will cry 'ball!' in anticipation of the umpire awarding the free kick.

interchange players—The players of the team (in senior football usually restricted to three) who are off the ground but available for unlimited substitution during the game. Substitutions may take place only through a designated interchange area on the boundary line controlled by an interchange steward.

kickoff—When a player from a defending team kicks the ball back into play after a behind has been scored.

kickoff lines—The lines of the goal square.

knock on—Where a player does not attempt to pick up the ball but hits it to advantage. It must not be thrown or scooped.

lead—A player running to a free space and making a target for a teammate to footpass the ball.

loose man—A player who is not being checked by an opponent. Once teams have taken possession of the ball they will try to create a loose man by running off their opponents.

man up—Where a player is given the responsibility to cover a particular player when the opposition has gained possession of the ball.

mark—Where the ball has been caught on the full from a kick that has travelled at least 10 metres and has not been touched by any other player.

minor score—Another name given (often by television or radio commentators) for a behind worth 1 point.

off hands/off the pack—Where the ball is taken on the full as it falls free from a pack of players competing for a mark. Sometimes it is said that the ball is 'crumbed', and players who specialise in this skill are called 'crumbers'.

on the ball—Players who follow the ball around the ground rather than being placed in a set position are said to be 'on the ball'. These are usually the ruckman, ruck rover and rover.

on the full—A free kick is awarded to the opposition whenever a team kicks the ball over the boundary line on the full—that is, without first bouncing in the field of play.

oval—The playing field. Usually grassed and with dimensions of between 110 to 155 metres in width and between 135 to 185 metres in length.

over the mark—A defensive player standing a mark or a free kick will be directed where to stand by the central umpire. If he encroaches over that mark before the ball is kicked he will be penalised 50 metres for being 'over the mark'.

pack—A group of players contesting the ball in the air.

palming—The ruckman trying to direct the ball from a hit out to one of his teammates.

play on—Where a player elects not to go back behind his mark after a mark or free kick but to get the ball quickly to advantage to a teammate. Any time after the umpire calls 'play on!' the player is able to be tackled and if tackled will have been deemed to have had sufficient time to dispose of the ball and will be penalised for holding the ball.

pocket—The areas on the field close to the behind posts.

propping—A player stopping in front of and facing an opponent, forcing him to make his move or dispose of the ball.

push and run—If the ball is within 5 metres a player may push off his opponent (but not in the back or the face).

rocket handball—A handball where the ball spins end over end backwards in flight. It is the preferred method for accuracy and distance.

runner—A team official who carries messages from the coach to players during the course of the game. There are no time-outs in Australian football.

running off—Usually refers to defensive player leaving his opponent to provide a running attacking option into attack for his team. Coaches will despair if the forward player doesn't chase his defensive opponent and fight to keep the ball in the attacking zone.

shepherding—A player using his body to block an opponent from the ball or a teammate. It is illegal to shepherd more than 5 metres from the ball.

smother—Where a player uses his hands to trap the ball on an opponent's foot as he kicks.

spoil—A defensive action where the ball is punched away from an opponent attempting to mark.

standing the mark—The player standing on the spot where his opponent has marked the ball or been given a free kick for an infringement. He does this to ensure that his opponent does not play on and has to kick over the mark, which is a more controlled situation for the defensive team to counter.

tackle—A player with the ball can be grabbed above the knees and below the shoulders.

tagging—Shadowing an opponent over the field with the sole object of denying him possession of the ball.

Usually the player given this defensive responsibility must sacrifice his own attacking game.

taking the ball—Gathering the bouncing ball in the hands prior to a controlled disposal to a teammate.

throw-in—When the ball has gone out of bounds over the boundary line (other than a kick on the full or directly from a kickoff), the boundary umpire will throw the ball back into play over his head towards the centre of the ground.

torpedo punt—A kick where the ball spirals through the air.

tumble pass—A handball where the ball tumbles end over end forwards in flight. If it goes to ground it will bounce away from the player.

turnover—Losing possession of the ball to the opposition team.

About the Author

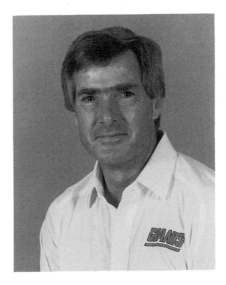

From representing South Australia as a school-boy and amateur footballer to serving as fitness coach for the South Australian team that won the 1988 and 1993 Australian championships, Trevor Jaques has been involved in Australian football most of his life. He has played, taught and coached at all levels, serving in the capacity of fitness coach at the elite level for over 20 years. This experience led him to become fitness director, runner and team selector for the Adelaide Football Club in the Australian Football League, positions he has held since the team's inception in 1991.

Trevor received his bachelor's degree from Adelaide University in 1975 and his master's degree from Michigan State University in 1982. As a senior lecturer in sport science at the University of South Australia, he teaches sports and skills analysis, sports injuries and football. Trevor resides in Adelaide, South Australia with his wife, Trudie, and their two daughters. His extensive travels have taken him to 27 countries, a highlight being trekking and rafting in Nepal. Besides travelling, Trevor enjoys snow skiing, reading and music and is an avid fan of American football.